Introducing Vala Programming

A Language and Techniques to Boost Productivity

Michael Lauer

Apress®

Introducing Vala Programming: A Language and Techniques to Boost Productivity

Michael Lauer
Neu-Isenburg, Hessen, Germany

ISBN-13 (pbk): 978-1-4842-5379-3   ISBN-13 (electronic): 978-1-4842-5380-9
https://doi.org/10.1007/978-1-4842-5380-9

Managing Director, Apress Media LLC: Welmoed Spahr
Acquisitions Editor: Steve Anglin
Development Editor: Matthew Moodie
Coordinating Editor: Mark Powers
Technical Reviewer: Rico Tzschichholz

Cover designed by eStudioCalamar

Cover image designed by Freepik (www.freepik.com)

Distributed to the book trade worldwide by Springer Science+Business Media New York, 233 Spring Street, 6th Floor, New York, NY 10013. Phone 1-800-SPRINGER, fax (201) 348-4505, e-mail orders-ny@springer-sbm.com, or visit www.springeronline.com. Apress Media, LLC is a California LLC and the sole member (owner) is Springer Science + Business Media Finance Inc (SSBM Finance Inc). SSBM Finance Inc is a **Delaware** corporation.

For information on translations, please e-mail editorial@apress.com; for reprint, paperback, or audio rights, please email bookpermissions@springernature.com.

Apress titles may be purchased in bulk for academic, corporate, or promotional use. eBook versions and licenses are also available for most titles. For more information, reference our Print and eBook Bulk Sales web page at http://www.apress.com/bulk-sales.

Any source code or other supplementary material referenced by the author in this book is available to readers on GitHub via the book's product page, located at www.apress.com/9781484253793. For more detailed information, please visit http://www.apress.com/source-code.

Printed on acid-free paper

For my wonderful family: Klothilde, Hans, Gaby, Sabine,
and Lara-Marie.

Table of Contents

About the Author

Michael "Mickey" Lauer is a freelance software architect and author living in Neu-Isenburg, Germany. He is a free-software-enthusiast who enjoys solving problems with mobile and distributed systems. Learn more on his personal web site: www.vanille.de.

CHAPTER 1

Introduction

In the beginning, the Universe was created. This has made a lot of people very angry and been widely regarded as a bad move.

—Douglas Adams, The Hitchhiker's Guide to the Galaxy

This chapter explains why Vala is a good idea and how you could benefit from a massively increased productivity, if you use it. It talks a bit about the history of Vala and mentions the author's personal involvement. Structure, audience, and typographic conventions are presented.

Why Vala?

Throughout the last decades, software development has been subject to a gradual but significant shift in priorities. Whereas in former times the *run-time performance* of a program was the most important aspect, these days, the *build-time performance*—the time required to transfer a problem description into a running program—is becoming more and more relevant. The build-time performance not only depends on the initial effort for writing a program but also includes the time required for debugging and maintenance, which is usually significantly higher compared to the initial writing.

© Michael Lauer 2019
M. Lauer, *Introducing Vala Programming*, https://doi.org/10.1007/978-1-4842-5380-9_1

The figure below shows some of the more common languages with respect to their run-time and build-time efficiency.

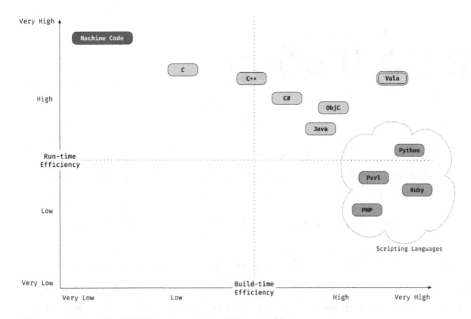

Figure 1-1. *Build-Time vs. Run-Time Efficiency*

One of the main factors that play into the run-time and build-time performance of a program written in a certain programming language is the language's *level of abstraction*. Low-level programming languages support a direct mapping of instructions to machine code (the *native* language to the CPU). This results in a speedy run-time performance but generally requires a higher implementation effort. Examples for languages with a low level of abstraction are *C* and *Assembler*, they belong to the oldest programming languages.

The widespread use of computer programs in almost every aspect of human life has lead to an increasing complexity of software systems. In light

of the rapid advances in processing power,[1] this complexity can be handled
by creating higher levels of abstractions in programming languages. High-
level programming languages allow to formulate algorithms in a more
natural way, reducing the time to solve a problem and making it easier to
read, understand, debug, and maintain. Considering that the programming
costs are often a major factor when creating a new software system, this
allows for significant economic advantages. Examples for languages with
a high level of abstraction are *Python and Ruby*—also called *scripting
languages* or sometimes 4GLs *(fourth-generation languages)*.

A high level of abstraction comes with a more complex translation of a
program's *source code* into machine code—instructions can no longer be
directly mapped, but even simple statements can lead to tens, hundreds,
or even thousands of generated machine code instructions. Writing
compilers for such languages is a complex task. A way to simplify this is
to use the *interpreter* concept, where a program no longer gets directly
translated into machine code but into an *intermediate representation,*[2]
sometimes called *bytecode*, which then gets executed by a special
program—an interpreter or a *virtual machine (VM)*.

Compared to a "real" CPU, a virtual machine, such as the *JAVA virtual
machine (JVM)*, provides an execution environment at a much higher
level—on the expense of a slower run-time and increased memory
requirements.[3]

---

[1]Moore's law of doubling the transistor density in integrated circuits approximately
every two years has been valid for five decades. By now, physical boundaries
make it almost impossible for it to continue, which is why the development has
shifted toward massive parallelization instead of ever-growing clock rates.

[2]Many compilers are using a similar scheme, e.g., gcc and clang are separated into
a *frontend* and a *backend.* The frontend is generating architecture independent
code; the platform-specific backend creates the resulting machine code.

[3]Although *just-in-time compilation (JIT)* techniques can help here, the general
statement still holds.

This situation gets tightened with the vast success of today's mobile platforms, such as "smartphones," "tablets," or "smart home" gadgets for the *Internet of Things (IOT)*. In contrast to stationary systems, mobile systems come with severe resource constraints. Battery efficiency is very important. On the other hand though, any recent (networked) GUI application contains an intrinsic level of complexity that is best handled by employing a programming language with a sufficiently high abstraction level.

For a programming language, run-time performance and build-time performance are often conflicting demands. It is very hard to optimize for both, so usually you have to decide on one.

The programming language *Vala* has been created to get the "best of both worlds": Vala combines the high-level build-time performance of scripting languages with the run-time performance of low-level programming languages.

Vala provides modern language features, such as

- Object-oriented programming (OOP) with interfaces, (abstract) classes, and polymorphism

- Type inference

- Structured exception handling

- Lambda functions and closures

- Asynchronous coroutines

- Automatic memory handling based on reference counting and ownership rules

- Loose coupling with signals

- Interfaces and delegates

- Pre- and postconditions

- And more

Vala implements these language features by relying on the `glib` library created by the GNOME project. Thus, the availability of that library on your chosen platform is a prerequisite for everything but the most trivial Vala program.[4]

The syntax of Vala is inspired by *C#* and should look very familiar to everyone with previous experience in any imperative language. While Vala is not an interpreted language, it is not directly compiled into machine code either. The Vala compiler generates an intermediate representation, which, in this case, is *ANSI-C*.[5]

This has several advantages:

1.   Vala uses the `C` compiler (these days usually `gcc` or `clang`), which is a widespread and excellently maintained compiler available for many platforms.

2.   The generated `C` code can be shipped and compiled even on systems where Vala itself might not be available.

3.   Libraries written in Vala feature a C-API[6] and can be used everywhere where C libraries can be used.

4.   C-Libraries are very easy to integrate in Vala.

Of course, there are also some disadvantages:

1.   Compiling a Vala program invokes two compilers and hence takes longer than compiling a program "directly" written in C.

---

[4]In March 2018, the so-called "POSIX profile"—a way to create Vala programs that do not depend on glib—has been reintroduced to Vala.

[5]This may sound slightly familiar to the older ones among us: The first compiler for the *C++* programming language was called `cfront` and generated ANSI-C as well. *Objective-C* did start its career as a frontend for C as well.

[6]And also a *C-ABI (Application Binary Interface)*, which may be even more important for some use cases.

2. When the generated C code—for whatever reason—cannot be compiled, the developer will see a C compiler error which makes it hard to track back to the incorrect part of the originating Vala program.

3. Debugging Vala programs can sometimes be hard, if the debugger lacks support for Vala and you have to step into the generated C code.

While the first disadvantage is intrinsic to the current implementation of Vala (and is unlikely to change any time soon), the latter ones are more a matter of the immature state of the tooling—hence are likely to become less relevant in the future.

Vala is completely free and open source. The compiler is available under the *GNU Lesser General Public License (LGPL)* and supports the most common operating systems, such as Linux, macOS, BSD, and Windows. This license does not affect programs created with the Vala compiler—for your own programs, you're free to select any license that fits your project.

A Brief Take on History

Vala was created in 2006 by the Swiss computer science students *Jürg Billeter* and *Raffaele Sandrini*, who were rooted in the GNOME community and dreamed of a higher level alternative for developing UI applications in C. They did like the syntax and semantics of C# but did not want to use Mono.[7] After bootstrapping the initial project with C, only one year later (with release 0.1.0 in July 2007), the Vala compiler was *self-hosted*, that is, written in Vala itself.

---

[7]The major reasons for that likely being Mono's reliance on a VM and its nonexistent interoperability with arbitrary C-libraries.

6

In parallel to working on compiler stability and more language features, enhancing the functionality using *bindings* to other C-based libraries became an important task.

The period between 2008 and 2010 was most probably the "golden years" for Vala. As more and more (GNOME) community projects adopted Vala, it gained many users, some of them which also became contributors to the language itself. Development was quick, and some of the larger features, such as support for *DBus, closures,* and *asynchronous methods,* were implemented.

This was the time when the word of Vala leaked outside of the GNOME community and got attention by commercial vendors, who recognized the immense potential for saving time and money when writing Vala instead of C-based programs. Some of those vendors then started funding the Vala project—most notably *Nokia,* who were using Vala as part of their *Maemo* (later *MeeGo*) SDK for mobile devices.

In February 2011 though, Nokia and Microsoft jointly announced a major business partnership between the two companies, which eventually resulted in Nokia adopting *Windows* Phone as the primary platform for its future smartphones, thus replacing both Symbian and MeeGo. This led to Nokia cancelling most of the funding for GNOME projects, including Vala. In subsequent events, Jürg Billeter dropped out as the lead developer, and over the next couple of years, Vala lost a lot of traction.

For many months, the sole contributions happened in the bindings to other libraries, whereas the core stayed pretty much unchanged. The remaining Vala users got more and more annoyed about long-standing unresolved issues, such as when non-compilable C code is generated for a seemingly valid Vala program.

2015 was probably the worst year, as there were very little commits to the Vala source repository and almost no traffic on the mailing list. Many developers claimed that Vala was dead.

For some reason though, this changed in early 2016, when a small group of people started to tackle unresolved issues with the strong goal of releasing a stable version *1.0* in the "near" future. This in turn motivated further developers to "come back" and help—and at the time of writing this (August 2019), the commit ratio has reached a healthy state again. Both the Vala contributors and users have regained faith that the long-awaited 1.0 will eventually see the light of day.

A Personal Note

My first encounter with Vala was on the Linux-fair OpenExpo 2007 in Zurich/Oerlikon, Switzerland, where I met its father Jürg Billeter and some of the first contributors. Having very recently worked on C and GObject-based applications, I was immediately attracted by the language's syntax and goals and promised myself to use it as soon as possible in one of my projects.

Three months later, I rewrote a graphical terminal emulator for the Openmoko smartphone platform using Vala and was *very* satisfied with how it turned out. Here's an excerpt of my blog post (taken from here) as of December 2007:

> *I just rewrote the* `openmoko-terminal2` *application (a lightweight terminal for the Openmoko environment using Vte) in Vala. [...]*
>
> *In my opinion, Vala is nothing more and nothing less than the future of application coding for the GNOME platform. Vala combines a nice high-level syntax (modeled after C# and Java) using* `GObject` *as the object model and compiles straight away to plain 'ole C. Yes, that means no runtime libraries, no bloat, no performance drawbacks.*

Vala removes the need of typing run time typecasts and endless function names and adds compile-time type checking. This will boost your coding-efficiency a lot. Vala has an enormous potential for the C-dominated GNOME platform and I hope people will realize that and be giving Vala a chance. [...]

After having gained a bit more experience with Vala, it became my language of choice for the second reference implementation of the freesmartphone.org special interest middleware. Although its development has stalled since 2011, it is still one of the largest projects ever written in Vala. During its development, I contributed a lot to Vala, in particular to asynchronous closures, DBus, and bindings to *Posix* and *Linux* low-level system and networking facilities, since all of these were strong requirements for the middleware I wrote.

Since I loved the language so much, I had the idea of spreading the word by the means of publishing an introductory book on Vala in 2008—more than ten years ago. Back then though I wanted to wait for "a while" to synchronize the publishing with the release of Vala 1.0—which I had expected for 2009 or 2010 at the latest. I really didn't think that it would take over a decade for this to happen, but I'm glad that Vala is still "alive and kicking," and given its ups and downs in the past ten years, this book is more important than ever.

Audience

This book is for developers with basic programming experience, preferably for those who already wrote programs using the GNOME libraries—either in C or using higher level languages with bindings. It is *not* an introduction into programming or algorithms.

Those coming from C#, Java, or Mono will feel right at home with the syntax and hopefully fall in love with the run-time performance and wide access to external libraries.

In principle though, anyone who is developing for Windows, macOS, or Unix-like platforms and wants to increase his or her productivity with Vala should find something useful in this book.

Overview

The remaining chapters are structured as follows:

Chapter 2: Getting Started gets you from installing Vala to writing the first example program.

Chapter 3: Syntax and Semantics discusses the basic set of rules for the Vala programming language.

Chapter 4: Object-Oriented Programming shows how to write interfaces and classes, and introduces the signal concept for the loose binding of components.

Chapter 5: Networking presents network communication using Vala—from plain sockets to HTTP.

Chapter 6: IPC with DBus details how to communicate with other processes on your local machine.

Chapter 7: UI with GTK+ concentrates on writing event-driven applications with graphical user interfaces.

Chapter 8: Linux Programming explains how to use Linux-specific system APIs.

Chapter 9: Bindings shows how to use external C code by writing Vala bindings.

Typographical Conventions

The following typographical conventions are used in this book:

- *Italics* introduces new terms.

- `Constant width` indicates a piece of code, a tool or library, or file name.

- Lines starting with a $ refer to a shell command-line prompt.

Longer code examples are often contained in constant width code blocks such as

```c#
void doSomething() { // empty }
```

When presenting code snippets, they are usually *prepended* by the rough idea and motivation for why the snippet is necessary and *followed* by a detailed discussion of the individual statements.

Source Code

While it can be instructive to follow the presented snippets by typing them into an editor, you can also just copy and paste the relevant bits or refer to the repository accompanying this book. The source code presented in this book is available via the Download Source Code button located at `www.apress.com/9781484253793`, or from `https://github.com/mickeyl/introduction-to-vala`.

CHAPTER 2

Getting Started

Thank you for making a simple door very happy.

—Douglas Adams, The Hitchhiker's Guide to the Galaxy

In the sense of the tradition founded by *Kernighan and Ritchie*,[1] we start with the obligatory "Hello World" program—a minimal example that not only provides a first look at the syntax but also discusses *the Vala way* from the source code to the executable binary. We also take a glance behind the curtain to see how Vala operates in the background and translates your program into C.

Installing

Before being able to use Vala, you need to install it on your computer, of course. The actual source for the Vala compiler depends on your operating system. If you're on a variant of BSD or a Linux distribution, you will usually want to use the distribution's package manager to install Vala. Make sure that you have at least Vala version *0.46.0*—which is the current

---

[1]Brian W. Kernighan, Dennis M. Ritchi: C Programming Language. Prentice Hall, 1978. ISBN 978-0131101630.

© Michael Lauer 2019
M. Lauer, *Introducing Vala Programming*, https://doi.org/10.1007/978-1-4842-5380-9_2

development version at the time of writing. Note that there's also a long term support branch (currently at version *0.40.x*) available, if you're on a more conservative setup. If your installer does not provide a suitable package, please head over to the Vala home page to download the desired source package for manual compiling and installing.

FreeBSD

On FreeBSD, Vala is available from FreshPorts. To install the port:

```
1    $ cd /usr/ports/lang/vala/ && make install clean
```

To add the package:

```
1    $ pkg install vala
```

macOS

On macOS, you can use the Homebrew package manager to install Vala using

```
1    $ brew install vala
```

Windows

On Windows, packages are provided by the MSYS2 project. Begin with the MSYS2 installer and use pacman -S **package** to install the required packages. Depending on the processor architecture (64-bit vs. 32-bit), there are different packages.

For 64-bit Windows, the package architecture is given as x86_64. To install packages for 32-bit Windows, change x86_64 to i686.

To install Vala on 64-bit Windows:

```
1   $ pacman -S mingw-w64-x86_64-gcc
2   $ pacman -S mingw-w64-x86_64-pkg-config
3   $ pacman -S mingw-w64-x86_64-vala
```

Verifying the Correct Installation

To verify that you have a working Vala installation, please issue vala on the command line. You should see a prompt similar to

```
1   $ vala
2   No source file specified.
```

Let's write our first Vala program now.

Hello World

Launch your preferred text editor or IDE[2] and type in the following lines:

```
1   // helloWorld.vala
2
3   int main( string[] args )
4   {
5       stdout.printf( "Hello World!\n" );
6       return 0;
7   }
```

---

[2]Vala does not come bundled with a dedicated integrated development environment; however it will work with a generic one, like Eclipse or Anjuta. In addition, there is a small choice of Vala-specific IDEs, like Valama.

15

Save this in a file called helloWorld.vala, and then move over to a command-line prompt to issue vala helloWorld.vala. If you typed everything correctly, you should see

```
1   $ vala helloWorld.vala
2   Hello World!
```

Let's briefly discuss this first program:

```
1   // helloWorld.vala
```

The double slash // introduces a one-line *comment* in Vala that continues until the end of line. Another valid form for a comment is the inline-comment, for example, /* inline comment */. This kind of comment may span multiple lines.

```
1   int main( string[] args )
```

This starts a *function* definition. Functions in Vala can return at most one value—in this case an **int**eger—and accept an arbitrary number of *parameters*—in this case an array of strings. To denote an array with unspecified length, you append square brackets [] after the base type. Most functions in Vala need a body which is enclosed in curly braces {}.

```
1   stdout.printf( "Hello World!\n" );
```

With this line, we call the printf function (actually a *method*, in OOP speech) on the object stdout and give the string "Hello World!\n" as the parameter. String literals in Vala are enclosed in double quotes ("). Vala requires a semicolon (;) at the end of every *statement*.

```
1   return 0;
```

The **return** statement ends a function and (optionally) returns a value to the caller—in this case, the value 0.

This small program prints out the string *Hello World!* on the console streamed through the *standard output* pseudo-file stdout. The function definition **int** main(string[] args) maps to the standard entry point main() as defined by the *Portable Operating System Interface based on UNIX* (POSIX).

With this first program working, you can now proceed to the object-oriented variant of "Hello World" or read more about what happened behind the scenes when you invoked the Vala complier with vala helloWorld.vala.

Behind the Curtain

Calling the Vala compiler with the name vala is a convenient way to quickly try out a new program—similar to a scripting language. vala is usually just a *softlink* to the actual compiler, which is named valac. On the machine I'm using to write this, it looks like this:

```
1    $ ls -l `which vala`
2    lrwxr-xr-x  1 mickey  admin  9 29 Mar 10:23 /usr/local/bin/
     vala -> vala
        -0.46
```

When called as vala helloWorld.vala, the Vala compiler valac does the following in the background:

1. It reads the contents of helloWorld.vala into memory and analyzes your program.

2. It creates the corresponding C file helloWorld.c in a temporary folder.

3. It invokes the system's C compiler (e.g., gcc), which creates an executable helloWorld in a temporary folder.

4. It runs the executable helloWorld.

5. It removes the temporary folder including all temporary files.

If you are on a UNIX-like system and you would like to run Vala in a way that is even closer to a scripting language, you can insert the following at the very beginning of helloWorld.vala:

```
1  #!/usr/bin/env vala
```

The characters #! are the so-called UNIX Shebang, which instructs your *shell* (e.g., bash, dash, zsh) to call the specified command and feed it with the remainder of the file. If you then make the file *executable* via chmod a+rx helloWorld.vala, you can invoke it directly from the shell like this:

```
1  $ ./helloWorld.vala
2  Hello World!
```

To take a look behind the curtain, let's compile your example program with the following command:

```
1  $ valac --save-temps helloWorld.vala
```

Called with this command line, Vala will not run any executables but only compile the given input files. The command-line option --save-temps instructs valac not to remove any temporary files, so that we have a chance to inspect them:

```
1  $ ls -l
2  total 40
3  -rwxr-xr-x  1 mickey  staff  8524  1 Nov 14:32 helloWorld
4  -rw-r--r--  1 mickey  staff   526  1 Nov 14:32 helloWorld.c
5  -rwxr-xr-x@ 1 mickey  staff    81  1 Nov 11:46 helloWorld.vala
```

There's not much sense in viewing the helloWorld executable, since this is just the compiled binary, containing machine code for your target platform. The helloWorld.c file is another story though.

Occasionally, it can be instructive to view the contents of the generated C code.[3] Let's do this now. It should look somewhat similar to this:

```
1   $ cat helloWorld.c
2   /* helloWorld.c generated by valac 0.44.7, the Vala compiler
3    * generated from helloWorld.vala, do not modify */
4
5   #include <stdlib.h>
6   #include <string.h>
7   #include <glib.h>
8   #include <stdio.h>
9
10  gint _vala_main (gchar** args, int args_length1);
11
12  gint _vala_main (gchar** args, int args_length1) {
13      gint result = 0;
14      FILE* _tmp0_;
15      _tmp0_ = stdout;
16      fprintf (_tmp0_, "Hello World!\n");
17      result = 0;
18      return result;
19  }
20
21  int main (int argc, char ** argv) {
22      return _vala_main (argv, argc);
23  }
```

---

[3]I recommend to look into the generated C code from time to time. It can help not only for debugging some cases but also to enjoy seeing how many lines of codes you have saved by using Vala.

19

Even though this is a really trivial program, we can already observe a number of notable facts:

- Although we did not explicitly use anything from glib, its header files are #included by default.

- Vala creates its own main function _vala_main, which is using the glib variants of the standard C types, that is, **int** becomes gint and **char** becomes gchar.

- Vala's array of strings string[] is mapped into a gchar** with the array length being passed as a separate parameter args_length1.

- Vala's file object stdout is mapped to the POSIX *file descriptor* for stdout.

- Vala's printf method is nothing more than the good ole POSIX fprintf.

- The generated C code is *somewhat readable*, although it is littered with seemingly useless assignments to temporary variables. This is not so much visible in this small example, but feel free to inspect a larger program, and you will see *a lot* of _tmpX_ variables.

valac understands many more command-line options. Use valac --help or man valac to learn more about these.

Hello Object-World

Let us turn the example from the last section into an object-oriented "Hello World" program. Fire up your text editor and save the following listing into a file named helloObjectWorld.vala:

```
1    // helloObjectWorld.vala
2
3    class HelloWorld
4    {
5        private string name;
6
7        public HelloWorld( string name )
8        {
9            this.name = name;
10       }
11
12       public void greet()
13       {
14           var fullGreeting = "Hello " + this.name + "!\n";
15           stdout.printf( fullGreeting );
16       }
17   }
18
19   int main( string[] args )
20   {
21       var helloWorldObject = new HelloWorld( args[1] );
22       helloWorldObject.greet();
23       return 0;
24   }
```

Run this with vala helloObjectWorld.vala --run-args Mickey, and you should see

```
1    $ vala helloObjectWorld.vala --run-args Mickey
2    Hello Mickey!
```

This program takes your first command-line argument and prints out a personalized greeting. For this, we created a class that stores the argument in a private variable (in OOP speech, an *instance member*). Let's take a look at how we did this:

```
1    class HelloWorld
```

The **class** keyword introduces a class declaration. Class declarations require an implementation block { ... }.

```
1    private string name;
```

This statement declares an instance member named name with the type string. Instance members are variables held *per instance*. They support an (optional) *access modifier*. **private** makes sure that the member will only be visible to code that is within this class declaration, that is, the said member cannot be accessed from the outside.

```
1    public HelloWorld( string name )
```

Inside a class declaration, you can define the class methods. Class methods are pretty much the same as functions, but they live in the *scope* of a class and can access member variables and all other methods defined in the same class. Class methods also feature an access modifier.

If you have paid attention, you will also have noticed two things:

1. This method definition is lacking a return value specification.

2. This method has the same name as the class it lives in.

This is the way to specify the *class constructor*, that is, the special method that gets executed when a caller creates a new instance of the class.

```
1    this.name = name
```

This statement copies the value of the name parameter into the class' member variable—which, in this case, happens to have the same name (this is not a requirement). If you want to refer to a member variable that has the same name as a variable in the current scope, you have to use the **this** to denote the current instance.[4]

```
1    public void greet()
```

The greet-method receives no arguments and returns no arguments. By using the visibility classifier **public**, we make it callable from outside the class.

```
1    var fullGreeting = "Hello " + this.name + "!\n";
```

This line composes the greeting string by declaring a new string variable and assigning its initial content. Until now, whenever we needed a variable, we declared its type *explicitly* (e.g., by specifying **string** or **int**). The keyword var instructs the Vala compiler to automatically *infer* the correct type for this variable by looking at the right-hand side of the assignment.

This feature is called *type inference* and will save you a lot of typing. It also can reduce visual clutter:

1. For longer type names, you would otherwise have to duplicate the type name, for example, when creating a new class instance (see the following).

2. Most of the time, the type of a variable is less relevant than its interface, that is, what methods it supports.

---

[4]Similar to C++, Java, and Objective-C, the **this** parameter is supplied as an invisible parameter when calling an instance's method. Some programming languages make this explicit in their method definition, i.e., Smalltalk's and Python's self parameter work this way.

As you can see, Vala supports *string concatenation* using the +
operator.[5] This is just one of many ways to construct a string though:

```
1    stdout.printf( fullGreeting );
```

This prints out the value of the fullGreeting string on stdout—same
as with the previous program.

In the main() function, we can see how a new instance of a class can
be created:

```
1    var helloWorldObject = new HelloWorld( args[1] );
```

The variable helloWorldObject is declared and initialized with a
new instance of the HelloWorld class—again, by the use of Vala's type
inference. If, for some reason, you wanted to state the type explicitly, in
this case, you could also have written:

```
1    HelloWorld helloWorldObject = new HelloWorld( args[1] );
```

The keyword **new** is responsible for creating a new instance. It also
calls the constructor with the specified arguments, in this case args[1],
which is the second value[6] of the string array args that gets passed into the
main() function:

```
1    helloWorldObject.greet();
```

To actually make something happen, we call the public greet method
on the newly created instance helloWorldObject. This method does not
take any parameters (of course, we could have also made it accept the
name as a string parameter instead of passing the value in the constructor
call; however, I just wanted to introduce member variables here).

---

[5]Vala does not support *operator overloading*.

[6]POSIX defines that the name of the executable is being passed as the first
parameter.

24

Watch out what happens, if you call this example without the necessary parameter. You should see something similarly to this:

```
1    $ vala helloObjectWorld.vala
2    ** (process:19026): CRITICAL **:
3        hello_world_construct: assertion 'name != NULL' failed
4    ** (process:19026): CRITICAL **:
5        hello_world_greet: assertion 'self != NULL' failed
```

We are seeing several *CRITICAL* run-time warnings here, issued by statements in the generated C code. (Feel free to have a look at that code now, be aware that, due to the use of classes, it is quite a mouthful.)

Obviously this program requires the name parameter to be unequal NULL (which corresponds to **null** in Vala)—this is due to Vala's *nullability* concept. For most types, Vala expects parameters to have a non-**null** value. To specify that **null** is a valid value for a parameter, you append the ? modifier to its type name. Let's do this now by changing the corresponding line in our last program to

```
1    public HelloWorld( string? name )
```

Running this leads to

```
1    $ vala ./helloObjectWorld.vala
2    Hello !
```

The run-time warnings are gone—although it might be better to catch this case by adding a check. Change the main() function to

```
1    int main( string[] args )
2    {
3        if ( args.length < 2 )
4        {
5            stderr.printf( "Usage: %s <name>\n", args[0] );
6            return -1;
```

```
7          }
8          var helloWorldObject = new HelloWorld( args[1] );
9          helloWorldObject.greet();
10         return 0;
11     }
```

Saving this to a file helloObjectWorld2.vala and then running it without the necessary argument now leads to

```
1    $ vala helloObjectWorld2.vala
2    Usage: helloObjectWorld2.vala <name>
```

We did this by adding an **if** clause that inspects the length of the array passed in the parameter args:

```
1    if ( args.length < 2 )
```

If clauses require a *predicate* (a boolean function that resolves to *true* or *false*)—in this case we're comparing the length instance variable of the array with the number 2 to check whether we have enough parameters to continue:

```
1    stderr.printf( "Usage: %s <name>\n", args[0] );
```

If the boolean condition evaluates to **true**, we don't have enough command-line arguments; hence we send our complaint to stderr—which is the dedicated pseudo-file object for error messages. The actual error message is a parametrized string conforming to the POSIX sprintf(3) type definition. Read more on the possible format specifiers with man sprintf on the command line.

If you have paid attention to the last footnote, you have already learned that POSIX passes the number of the program as the first parameter; hence args[0] contains exactly that.

Hello GUI-World

It is time to do something more visual. The final variant of our "Hello World" program shows how to create an event-driven application with the GTK+ user interface library:

```vala
1    // helloGUIWorld.vala
2    int main( string[] args )
3    {
4        Gtk.init( ref args );
5
6        var window = new Gtk.Window();
7        window.title = "Hello UI World";
8        window.border_width = 10;
9        window.window_position = Gtk.WindowPosition.CENTER;
10       window.set_default_size( 400, 150 );
11       window.destroy.connect( Gtk.main_quit );
12
13       var button = new Gtk.Button.with_label( "Click me!" );
14       button.clicked.connect( () => {
15           button.label = "Thank you!";
16       } );
17
18       window.add( button );
19       window.show_all();
20
21       Gtk.main();
22       return 0;
23   }
```

Save this to a file named helloGUIWorld.vala. Vala programs that include external library functionality have to declare this at the time of compilation, using the --pkg command-line argument, followed by the name of the library. To compile and run this program, you would usually do this as follows:

```
1    $ vala --pkg=gtk+-3.0 helloGUIWorld.vala
```

If this fails with a fatal error: 'gtk/gtk.h' file not found, you are missing the development headers of the GTK+-3 library. Please install them with your operating system's package manager and try again.

When the compilation command succeeds, you should be able to see a new top-level window being opened on your desktop containing a clickable button labelled "Click me!" as shown in Figure 2-1.

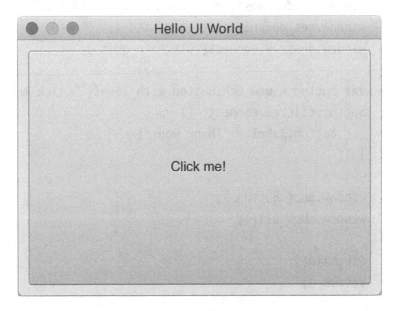

Figure 2-1. *Application Created by helloGUIWorld.vala*

Clicking that button changes its text to "Thank you!". Closing the window should exit the program. Let's discuss how we did this:

```
1   int main( string[] args )
```

The main function is completely identical to the previous examples:

```
1   Gtk.init( ref args )
```

This is the first actual use of the GTK+ library. GTK+ comes with a *namespace*, which is a Vala construct to structure programs. Namespaces can contain all kinds of declarations and are nestable. The . operator is used to reference an entity in a namespace.

Before using anything in a GTK+ GUI application, you need to initialize the library. Call init() and submit the array of command-line arguments that you got from main() as the parameter. Note that we are using the ref keyword here; this indicates that the parameters are called by reference, which allows the calling function to manipulate them. Read more on parameter passing in Chapter 3.

```
1   var window = new Gtk.Window();
```

Here, we instantiate a Gtk.Window object, which represents a top-level window.

```
1   window.title = "Hello UI World";
2   window.border_width = 10;
3   window.window_position = Gtk.WindowPosition.CENTER;
4   window.set_default_size( 400, 150 );
```

These four statements configure the top-level window by specifying a title, a border width, a window position, and a default size.[7] Note that Gtk.WindowPosition is an enum (an enumeration with named constants) defined in the Gtk namespace and CENTER is one of its values:

```
1    window.destroy.connect( Gtk.main_quit );
```

This clause specifies what should happen when the window manager signalizes that the top-level window has been destroyed, for example, by someone closing it. This is done by connecting a function—in this case Gtk.main_quit, which instructs GTK+ to leave the *mainloop* entered by Gtk.main() (see the following).

The method connect() is actually part of something bigger: The *signal* mechanism in Vala, which implements callbacks for loosely connected components. Not to be confused with UNIX signals, a Vala signal allows connecting application-specific events with one or more *listeners*:

```
1    var button = new Gtk.Button.with_label( "Click me!" );
```

Here, an instance of Gtk.Button, which represents a *push button*, is created. As you may remember, to instantiate a new object, you have to call its constructor. Vala classes can have multiple constructors. Button.with_label is a constructor for Gtk.Button with a string parameter, setting the label of the push button:

```
1    button.clicked.connect( () => {
2            button.label = "Thank you!";
3    } );
```

To make something happen when the button gets clicked, we could write another method and connect it to the clicked signal. Since such a function will only be called on behalf of a user event, there is no other

---

[7]Note that these properties are merely hints to the *window manager* on your chosen platform; hence they may or may not be respected.

caller for it. Thus, we don't actually need a name for it and may as well create an *anonymous* function—also called *lambda function*. The general syntax for Vala's lambda functions is (parameter list)=> { implementation block }. Within the implementation block for this function, we change the button's label to the string "Thank you":

```
1    window.add( button );
```

Calling add() on a top-level window hooks a GTK+ UI element into the widget hierarchy:

```
1    window.show_all();
```

By default, newly added UI elements are invisible by default. With the method show_all(), you can ensure that the newly added button will be visible:

```
1    Gtk.main();
```

The main() function in the Gtk namespace is a convenient way to create a new *mainloop* and start processing events. This function will only return after the mainloop has quit, for example, by calling main_quit() (see earlier text):

```
1    return 0;
```

This submits the return code 0 (success) to the calling shell.

This closes the discussion of your first GTK+ program written in Vala. Congratulations for making it this far! Event-driven UI applications are a huge topic and one of the major reasons for using Vala—we'll cover more of it in Chapter 7.

One closing word about namespaces: You have seen that we had to reference to every entity in the Gtk namespace fully qualified with the prefix Gtk. If you don't want to do this, you might as well consider the using directive:

```
1    using Gtk;
```

With this statement, we instruct Vala to "import" all declarations from the Gtk namespace into the global namespace, so that we can use them without prefixing. Whether to do this or not mostly depends on your style. Obviously you are saving yourself some typing; however you are losing the capability to see which namespace a certain element comes from. Resisting against using can also help to prevent ambiguous symbol errors, for example, between GLib.Menu and Gtk.Menu. Then again, a number of using directives at the top of every file might be useful for a quickly glancing which of the external libraries are being used.

Summary

We have presented three variants of the obligatory "Hello World" program. In the first variant, you have seen a function definition and learned how to work with variables. The second variant introduced a class declaration and explained how to instantiate an object of that class. The last variant showed how to use the GTK+ external library to create "Hello World" in an interactive UI fashion.

CHAPTER 3

Syntax and Semantics

'Ford!', he said. 'There's an infinite number of monkeys outside who want to talk to us about this script for Hamlet they've worked out.'

—Douglas Adams, The Hitchhiker's Guide to the Galaxy

This chapter provides more information about the basic Vala programming rules, including syntax and semantics of most language constructs. We will also cover some of the more common idioms. If you're coming from another language, this is the chapter that will get you up to speed. Since it might not be the most exciting chapter in this book, feel free to only glance through and come back whenever you need more information about a certain construct.

© Michael Lauer 2019

M. Lauer, *Introducing Vala Programming*, https://doi.org/10.1007/978-1-4842-5380-9_3

Basic Rules

Files

Vala recognizes three kinds of input files, *source code* files, *API* files, and *dependency* files:

> **Source Code**: Vala programs are written in UTF8-encoded text files with the extension `.vala`. The code contained within should confirm with the syntax rules as define by Vala's grammar.

> **API**: Vala API descriptions (from now on *VAPI*) contain interfaces to (external) libraries and are written in UTF8-encoded text files with the extension `.vapi`. VAPI files can be handwritten, created by helper programs, such as `vapigen`, or created as part of the Vala compilation process—the latter being helpful when your project creates a library that should be usable from other C or Vala programs.

> **Dependency**: Entities declared in a Vala API descriptions may refer to entities contained in other `.vapi` files. In that case, a `.deps` file with the same base name as the `.vapi` needs to be created, which lists all dependencies. For example, `linux.vapi` refers to structures defined in `posix.vapi`; hence `linux.deps` contains the string `posix`. Think of it as implicit `--pkg=...` arguments for `valac`.

Figure 3-1 shows how these (and other intermediate) file types relate to each other.

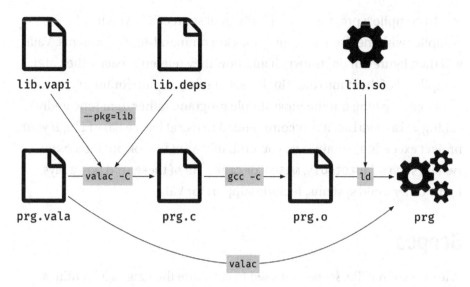

Figure 3-1. *Vala File Types*

While you may spend most of your time with source code files, inspecting the VAPI files that come with the Vala distribution can be helpful. They are a good source to discover the API for certain entities. You might also have a look at the official Vala Online Documentation.

Writing VAPI files is only necessary for accessing a library from Vala that does not have a VAPI file yet. You will learn more about writing bindings in Chapter 9.

Similar to scripting languages, Vala does not differentiate between header and implementation files. In contrast to languages like Java, Vala does not enforce a naming, directory, or file structure for your .vala files. There are no rules how classes or namespaces need to be organized.

You should not feel encouraged to lump all your classes into one big source file though. You should come up with a sane granularity and structure. The Vala compiler's source code itself may serve as an inspiration.

To compile a program out of individual source files, you invoke the compiler with the list of all source files as command-line arguments. Vala will then figure out on its own, if and how they reference each other, and compile all of them into one single executable program (or library).

For everything but the most simple program, rather than repeatedly calling vala or valac, it is recommended to use at least a Makefile. If your project exceeds a certain size, you probably want to look out for a *build system*, such as autotools, meson, or cmake. All of these, and nowadays many other build systems, include support for Vala.

Scopes

Within a source file, *scopes* are used to structure the language's entities (such as namespaces, classes, methods, and code blocks). A scope is defined using curly braces { and }. Scopes also delimit the *lifetime* of *variables*. Consider this code block:

```
1   {
2       int x;
3       var y = x; // valid, inside the scope
4   }
5
6   var y = x; // invalid, outside the scope
```

Scopes can be nested. When referring to an entity, the compiler always tries to start looking up the entity in the current scope. If it doesn't find it, it tries the next outer scope, and so on.

Due to this order, referring to an entity in an outer scope is always possible from an inner scope, however not otherwise:

```
1  {
2      int x;
3      {
4          int y = x; // valid, x is visible here
5      }
6
7      int x = y; // invalid, y does not exist here
8  }
```

While they don't make a lot of sense, empty scopes are also allowed.

Identifiers

Almost all of the Vala's language entities need to have a valid name before you can refer to them. This name is called *identifier* and is defined by the following rules:

1. You may use *any* combination of lowercase letters (a-z), uppercase letters (A-Z), underscores (_), and digits (0-9).

2. To define or refer to an identifier with a name that starts with a digit or is a Vala *keyword*, you must preface it with the @ character. This character is not considered a part of the name but merely used to disambiguate.

Interestingly, this set of rules is less restrictive compared to how other languages treat identifiers, that is, you are allowed to have an identifier starting with a digit or even an identifier which contains only digits. Albeit a bit strange in my opinion, the following is valid Vala code:

```
1  int @0 = 42;
2  stdout.printf( "%d", @0 );
```

Note   Due to requirements of the underlying implementation, Vala
class names need to have at least three characters.

Namespaces

A *namespace* is a structuring device used for combining language entities
that belong together. To put something into a namespace, you specify
the name of the namespace using the keyword namespace, followed by a
scope:

```
1    namespace MyNamespace
2    {
3        const int ANSWER_TO_EVERYTHING = 42;
4    }
```

A namespace may be divided over any number of source files but will
normally not be used outside of one project. To refer to an entity inside
a namespace, you have to prefix the entity's name with the name of the
namespace:

```
1    var x = MyNamespace.ANSWER_TO_EVERYTHING; // => 42
```

Alternatively, with the using directive, you can add a namespace to a
list of namespaces searched by the compiler when resolving an entity:

```
1    using MyNamespace;
2
3    var x = ANSWER_TO_EVERYTHING;
```

You are free to "import" multiple namespaces, even if they contain
a colliding entity. When you refer to such an entity though, you must
disambiguate by adding the fully qualified name. Consider the following
example with three files a.vala, b.vala, and c.vala:

```
1   // a.vala
2   namespace A
3   {
4       const int ANSWER_TO_EVERYTHING = 42;
5   }
```

```
1   // b.vala
2   namespace B
3   {
4       const int ANSWER_TO_EVERYTHING = 24;
5   }
```

```
1   // c.vala
2   using namespace A;
3   using namespace B;
4
5   int main()
6   {
7       stdout.printf( "Answer = %d", ANSWER_TO_EVERYTHING );
        // ambiguous reference
8   }
```

Trying to compile this, results in a nice and clear error:

```
1   $ valac -c a.vala b.vala c.vala
2   c.vala:6.32-6.51: error: `ANSWER_TO_EVERYTHING' is an
    ambiguous reference
3   between `A.ANSWER_TO_EVERYTHING' and `B.ANSWER_TO_
    EVERYTHING'
4       stdout.printf( "Answer = %d", ANSWER_TO_EVERYTHING );
5                                     ^^^^^^^^^^^^^^^^^^^^^
```

To fix this, refer to the constant fully qualified, that is, with A.ANSWER_
TO_EVERYTHING or B.ANSWER_TO_EVERYTHING.

Namespaces can be nested, either including one declaration within the other or by specifying the name in the form namespace A.B.

Note that the entities that appear in the top level of a file are put into an anonymous global namespace (sometimes also called *root* namespace). This namespace is always present and—in the case of disambiguating—can be referenced with global, followed by two colons (::):

```
1   const int a = 24;
2
3   namespace A
4   {
5       const int a = 42;
6       const int b = a; // => 42
7       const int c = global::a; // => 24
8   }
```

> **Note**   As mentioned in the introduction, Vala implements most of its language features using the glib library, which has all of its entities defined in the namespace GLib. Since this library is essential to Vala (and it would be both too cumbersome and almost unreadable having to preface everything with GLib.), its namespace is added to the lookup by default. You can imagine an invisible using GLib; residing on top of every source file.

Variables

Variables can be used to store values. Before using a variable with Vala, you have to either *declare* or *define* it. To declare a variable, you have to specify its *data type* and an identifier, which denotes its name, for example:

```
1   int x;
```

To define a variable, you have to use the assignment operator =:

```
1   string name = "Mickey";
```

Naturally, the definition of a variable implicitly declares it. Note that you may use the keyword var, if the type of the left-hand side can be inferred by inspecting the right-hand side:

```
1   var name = "Mickey";
```

Multiple variables can be defined or declared in one statement, separated by a comma (,):

```
1   int x, int y;
2   string foo = "foo", string bar = "bar";
```

Constants

To define *constant* values, you can use the keyword **const** before specifying the type:

```
1   const int ANSWER_TO_EVERYTHING = 42;
```

Note that with the current Vala compiler (0.44.7, at the time of writing), constant values cannot use type inference, that is, substituting var instead of an explicit type specifier is invalid.[1]

---

[1]This seems like an arbitrary limitation to me, which might be removed in future versions.

Enumerations

If you need to group a number of constants, you can use an *enumeration*. Enumerations map names to constant integer values:

```
1   enum EdgeType
2   {
3       LEFT,
4       TOP,
5       RIGHT,
6       BOTTOM
7   }
```

Similar to enumerations in other languages, you can either use automatic mapping or manually define them:

```
1   enum HttpStatusCode
2   {
3       OK = 200,
4       NOT_FOUND = 404
5   }
```

In Vala, enumerations are namespace-like, you need to refer to them fully qualified:

```
1   var leftEdge = EdgeType.LEFT;
```

In addition, Vala supports *flag type* enumerations, where the individual members are mapped to powers of 2. This way, a flag member only requires one bit of storage. Moreover, you can easily apply bitwise operators to test and combine flag type enumerations. To define a flag type enumeration, you annotate the enumeration with the [Flags] *code attribute*:

```
1   [Flags]
2   enum Borders
3   {
4       LEFT,
5       RIGHT,
6       TOP,
7       BOTTOM
8   }
```

As a convenient way of bit testing, flag type enumerators also support the in operator:

```
1   void drawBorders( Borders selectedBorders )
2   {
3       if ( selectedBorders & Borders.LEFT == Borders.LEFT )
4       {
5           // draw left border
6       }
7       if ( Borders.RIGHT in selectedBorders )
8       {
9           // draw right border
10      }
11      // ...
12  }
```

In contrast to many other languages, Vala enumerations can also contain functions. Such functions can be invoked either on an instance or the enum type itself.

The Type System

Vala's type system is based on *static typing* and *strong typing*, which means every variable has a (fixed, not implicitly convertible) type that is determined at compile time—either through type inference or static declaration.

Simple Types

Vala supports the usual set of basic types, as most other languages do:

Byte: 8-bit wide, signed (**char**) or unsigned (uchar)

Character: 32-bit Unicode character (unichar)

Integer: Platform-specific width, signed (**int**) or unsigned (uint)

Long Integer: Platform-specific width, signed (**long**) or unsigned (ulong)

Short Integer: Platform-specific width, signed (**short**) or unsigned (ushort)

Guaranteed-Size Integer: Width indicated by number prefix, signed (int8, int16, int32, int64) and unsigned (uint8, uint16, uint32, uint64)

Floating Point Number: Single precision (**float**) or double precision (**double**)

Boolean: Either **true** or **false**

Although these basic types are not part of the public *class hierarchy* in Vala (i.e., you can't inherit from any of those, and you don't need to instantiate them with **new**), they can be considered *pseudo-classes* in the sense that they can contain useful methods on "instance" or "class" scope.

Two of those methods are string to_string() and parse(string str). The former returns a string representation of the entity's value, and the latter parses a string representation and returns a value. Here's how to use them for integer values:

```
1   string x = 5.to_string(); // => "5"
2   int y = int.parse( "5" ); // => 5
```

Strings

A string in Vala is an immutable sequence of UTF8-encoded values. In addition to the standard string literal ("this is a string"), Vala also supports *verbatim strings*. These are strings in which escape sequences such as \t are not interpreted. Line breaks will be preserved, and quotation marks don't have to be masked. They are enclosed with triple double quotation marks:

```
1    string multiline = """Hello World.
2      This is a "verbatim string" using
3      multiple lines.""";
```

Strings are concatenated using the + operator. To construct a string at run-time, you can use printf():

```
1    var x = 5;
2    var myString = "%d".printf( x );
```

printf is a string "constructor" with an argument list of variable length. It accepts the POSIX sprintf(3) format specifiers, which—at run-time—will be replaced with the actual contents of the passed parameters.

String Templates An alternative to printf are *string templates*—strings prefaced with @, which evaluate embedded variables and expressions prefaced with $:

```
1    int a = 3;
2    int b = 2;
3    string s = @"$a * $b = $(a * b)";  // => "3 * 2 = 6"
```

45

You might wonder how this works without specifying the individual type information like in the call to `printf()`: Most of Vala's built-in types contain a `to_string()` method. This method returns a string representation of the type value. Here's an example for an enumeration:

```
1    enum Borders
2    {
3        LEFT,
4        RIGHT,
5        TOP,
6        BOTTOM
7    }
8
9    var x = Borders.LEFT;
10   stdout.printf( @"x = $x" ); // "x = BORDERS_LEFT"
```

Whether to use `printf` or string templates is merely a matter of style. Although slightly different C code is being generated for each of those, conceptually and performance-wise, they are very similar.

To compare the content of two strings, you can use the equality operator `==` or inequality operator `!=`.[2]

To access the individual characters of a string, the subscript operator `[]` can be used:

```
1    string str = "Hello World!";
2    unichar c = str[0]; // => 'H'
```

String Slicing Another handy feature Vala borrowed from scripting languages is *string slicing*, that is, extracting substrings from a string. The syntax is using the subscript operator plus a start index and an end

---

[2]In contrast to many compiled languages, Vala does not look at the memory address of the string but really scans through it character by character.

index for the substring range, for example, [start:end]. Note that both parameters are allowed to be negative—in this case the indices are relative to the *end* of the string:

```
1    string str = "Hello World!";
2    string substring1 = str[0:5]; // => "Hello"
3    string substring2 = str[1:-1]; // => "ello World";
```

Unfortunately, negative indices are only supported for slicing[3] and not for subscripting individual elements. Moreover, the common shorthand of leaving out the start or end parameter, like [4:] to get a substring with every character starting from the 5th element until the end or [:-2] to get a substring containing the last two characters, is not implemented (yet?).

Warning   Note that Vala's string subscript operator [ ] is mapped to its C equivalent, that is, for both subscripting and slicing, there is *no* run-time bounds checking. If you want to avoid run-time errors, you will have to perform the necessary checks on your own.

Arrays

An *array* is a sequence of variables of the same type. To declare an array, you add the brackets [ ] to the type name:

```
1    int[] arrayOfInts;
```

---

[3]In the current compiler version, support for negative indices is still somewhat broken; i.e., without referring to the length of the string, there is no invocation to get a substring containing exactly the last element.

Defining an array is done with the **new** operator. Here, we need to give it a concrete initial size:

```
1   arrayOfInts = new int[50];
```

To fill the array with values, you can add an initializer block with the element values. If you want to let Vala figure out the necessary size for the array, leave out the number in the type subscript:

```
1   var arrayOfInts = new int[] { 1, 2, 3 };
```

Note   If you already read some Vala source files, you might have stumbled over an alternative syntax. This statement compiles to the same code as the previous line:

```
1  int[] a = { 1, 2, 3 };
```

Unfortunately, type inference does not work here; thus you have to state the type *somewhere*, either on the left-hand side or on the right-hand side.

To access an individual entity in the array, once again, the subscript operator [ ] is used:

```
1   arrayOfInts[5] = 7;
2   stdout.printf( "5th element is %d", arrayOfInts[5] ); // =>
    "5th element is 7"
```

Warning   Let me remind you (again) that Vala's subscript operator
[ ] is directly mapped to its C equivalent, that is, there is *no* run-time
bounds checking. Unfortunately,[4] this also refers to the compile-time
checking of an array declaration. You can easily shoot yourself in the
foot by stating something (bogus) like

```
1    var arrayTooSmall = new int[1] { 1, 2, 3 };
```

This compiles to the following C code:

```
1    void _vala_main (void) {
2            gint* arrayTooSmall = NULL;
3            gint* _tmp0_;
4            gint arrayTooSmall_length1;
5            gint _arrayTooSmall_size_;
6            _tmp0_ = g_new0 (gint, 1);
7            _tmp0_[0] = 1; // ok
8            _tmp0_[1] = 2; // ERROR: out-of-bounds!
9            _tmp0_[2] = 3; // ERROR: out-of-bounds!
10           arrayTooSmall = _tmp0_;
11           arrayTooSmall_length1 = 1;
12           _arrayTooSmall_size_ = arrayTooSmall_length1;
13           arrayTooSmall = (g_free (arrayTooSmall), NULL);
14   }
```

Here, memory for the array pointed to by _tmp0_, is allocated with
g_new0, however only for *one* element. Thus, the consecutive assignments
of _tmp0_[1] and _tmp0_[2] are out-of-bounds, overwriting memory

---

[4]This looks like a *low hanging fruit*, which I hope can be fixed in a future version of
the compiler.

potentially allocated by other entities. While you might have *run-time luck* and this error will slip away unnoticed for some time, it is essentially a time-bomb.

The length of an array is available in the field length:

```
1   stdout.printf( "Array length = %d", arrayTooSmall.length );
// => " Array length = 1"
```

Similar to string operations, Vala supports slicing subarrays out of arrays:

```
1   int[] array = { 1, 2, 3, 4 };
2   var subarray = array[1:2]; // => { 2, 3 }
```

Appending an element to an array is supported with the += operator:

```
1   int[] array = { 1, 2, 3, 4 };
2   array += 5; // => { 1, 2, 3, 4, 5 }
```

If necessary, Vala will resize the array on your behalf. It does not allow concatenating two arrays though.

Multidimensional Arrays

Vala supports multidimensional arrays. Every comma (,) in the array type specifier adds an additional dimension. To declare a two-dimensional array:

```
1   var c = new int[3,4];
2   int[,] d = {{2, 4, 6, 8},
3               {3, 5, 7, 9},
4               {1, 3, 5, 7}};
5   d[2,3] = 42;
```

For multidimensional arrays, the length field itself becomes an array:

```
1   int[,] arr = new int[4,5];
2   int r = arr.length[0]; // => 4
3   int c = arr.length[1]; // => 5
```

Note that *arrays of arrays* (i.e., arrays with potentially heterogenous lengths) are not supported in Vala, since those cannot be represented by a contiguous block of memory. Moreover, multidimensional arrays do not support slicing or *flattening* (constructing a one-dimensional array out of a multidimensional one).

Structures

On top of these basic types, Vala supports a *compound* type that can be declared using the keyword struct. Structures are mutable, and by default all of their *fields* are publicly accessible. Here's an example of a struct named Vector representing a three-dimensional vector:

```
1   struct Vector
2   {
3       float x;
4       float y;
5       float z;
6   }
```

To create a new structure, you call its type name as if it was a function or method. You can then access the individual fields:

```
1   var a = Vector();
2   a.x = 1;
```

There's a shorthand for the initialization that allows specifying the initial field assignments in a block:

```
1    var a = Vector() { x=1, y=2, z=3 };
```

Note that partial initialization is also valid, that is, you don't *have* to specify every field. When creating a new instance, Vala allocates a zero-initialized contiguous memory block; hence, non-specified fields are initialized with zeroes.

In contrast to other languages, Vala structures can also contain functions:

```
1    struct Vector
2    {
3        float x;
4        float y;
5        float z;
6
7        public void reset()
8        {
9            x = y = z = 0;
10       }
11   }
```

Here we define the **public** function reset, which zeroes out all fields. By default, the visibility of functions in structs is **private**.

Note   The current implementation of the Vala compiler also accepts a **private** access modifier when you declare a structure field. It will emit a corresponding warning and ignore the modifier though, since fields in structs are always considered **public**.

Note that Vala structures belong to the value types; they are *stack allocated* and copied on assignment.

Classes

A *class* is a compound type that is supposed to combine data (member variables) and behavior (method implementations). A class can be defined using the keyword **class** and inherits data and behavior from a parent class, called *super class*. Here is a basic example:

```
1   class GeometricObject
2   {
3       public float x;
4       public float y;
5   }
6
7   class Rectangle : GeometricObject
8   {
9       public float width;
10      public float height;
11
12      public void paint();
13      {
14          // ...
15      }
16  }
```

Note that in contrast to structures, classes are reference types and as such are allocated on the heap.

Classes can be instantiated using the **new** operator with the name of the class as operand:

```
1   var rectangle = new Rectangle();
```

During instantiation, a *constructor* is being called (hence the parentheses), which can have an arbitrary number of parameters. Classes can have multiple constructors, although at least one must be present: If you don't define at least one constructor, an empty default constructor is automatically created when you declare a class.

While Vala does not support *multiple inheritance* (i.e., defining a class that has more than just one super class), you can declare one or more *interfaces* as *prerequisites*—thus creating a *mixin* (see the following).

Interfaces

An interface is a type similar to a class; however it cannot declare member variables and is not instantiable:

```
1    interface Drawable
2    {
3        public void draw();
4    }
```

The purpose of an interface is to specify an API contract which can then be used as prerequisite for other types. Here, we see the mixin DrawableRectangle which has Rectangle as base class and also claims to fulfill the Drawable interface:

```
1    class DrawableRectangle : Rectangle, Drawable
2    {
3        public void draw()
4        {
5            // implementation of draw method
6        }
7    }
```

An interface itself can also have one or more other interfaces as prerequisite(s).

Classes and interfaces are two major concepts of *object-oriented programming*, which we will cover in detail in the next chapter.

Delegates

A delegate is a *callable* type, that is, any function or method with a given parameter list (including the return type and any error specifications the method may have). Valid instances of a certain delegate are all functions that have a matching parameter list. Delegate types are declared with the keyword delegate:

```
1    delegate void VoidFuncTakingAnInt( int argument );
2
3    void concreteFunction( int bar)
4    {
5        // ...
6    }
7
8    int main()
9    {
10       VoidFuncTakingAnInt func = concreteFunction;
11       func( 5 );
12
13       return 0;
14   }
```

Warning   There is no type inference for delegates; hence you need to explicitly state the function or method name when defining or declaring a variable with a delegate type. If you forget to do this, the current implementation of the Vala compiler prints a non-helpful error message, such as

```
1   error: Assignment: Cannot convert from
    `concreteFunction' to ` concreteFunction'
```

Delegates are very useful for passing functions or methods around, in particular when used as *callbacks* in event-driven programming. Read more about that in Chapter 6.

Type Conversions

Vala supports two ways to convert between types—*implicit* and *explicit*:

Implicit Type Conversion: Compatible basic types are implicitly converted, when there is no loss of precision:

```
1   int x = 10.0; // error: Assignment: Cannot convert
    from `double' to ` int'
2   int y = 10;
3   double z = y; // ok
```

Explicit Type Conversion: Explicit type conversion can be enforced with *type casting*, that is, forcing the compiler to treat a given variable as if it were of another type:

```
1   int x = (int) 10.0; // ok
```

Warning   Static type casts are *not* checked at run-time. You can easily get run-time errors or crashes, if you're trying to convert noncompatible types.

Bug   The current version of the Vala compiler has a bug with some type casts, for example, trying to cast a `string` into a **double** with, for example, **double** x = (**double**)"Hello World"; is unfortunately accepted as Vala syntax but results in a C compiler error:

```
1    Untitled 5.vala.S4519Y.c:20:16: error: pointer
2        cannot be cast to type 'gdouble' (aka 'double')
3          x = (gdouble) "Hello World";
4                ^~~~~~~~~~~~~~~
```

Class types contain run-time type information, which allows for an additional form of type casting—read more about that in Chapter 4.

Operators

Vala supports the following general purpose operators:

Unary

! Logical not, can be applied to a boolean operand.

~ Bitwise not, can be applied to a numeric operand.

++, – Increment and decrement, can be applied to a numeric operand and assigned to left-hand side.

Binary

= Assignment, left-hand side must be an identifier; right-hand side must result in a value.

+, -, /, *, % Arithmetic, applied to left-hand side and right-hand side, resulting in a value.

+=, -=, /=, *=, %= Arithmetic assignment, applied to left-hand side and right-hand side, assigned to left-hand side.

|^, & Bitwise (OR, XOR, AND), applied to left-hand side and right-hand side, resulting in a value.

|=,^=, &= Bitwise assignment (OR, XOR, AND), applied to left-hand side and right-hand side, assigned to left-hand side.

», « Bitshift operators, shifting the left-hand side according to the right-hand side, resulting in a value.

»=, «= Bitshift assignment, shifting the left-hand side according to the right-hand side, assigning to the left-hand side.

== Equality operator, compares the left-hand with the right-hand side, resulting in a boolean value.

<, >, >=, <=, != Comparison operators, comparing the left-hand side with the right-hand-side, resulting in a boolean value.

?? Null coalescing operator, resulting in the left-hand side, if unequal **null**, else resolving to the right-hand side.

in Boolean containment operator, checking whether the left-hand side is a part of the right-hand side. This operator works on many sequences, for example, arrays and strings, flag type enumerations, and more collections that have a `contain()` method.

Ternary

?: Conditional operator, evaluates a condition and returns either the value of the left or the right subexpression based on whether the condition is **true** or **false**.

Special Purpose Operators

In addition to these general purpose operators (which support a variety of types), Vala has a few additional special purpose operators like is, typeof, and sizeof. These operators are limited to a smaller subset of types and/or use cases and will be discussed together with their respective type support in later chapters.

Vala does not support *overloadable* operators, that is, it is impossible to change the implementation of an operator or add custom type support. There is, however, a bit of *syntactic sugar* in the way that Vala recognizes a handful of methods with certain signatures as enabling operator support:

> **Subscripting**: Index access obj[index] and assignment obj[index] = item are mapped to the methods ItemType get(IndexType index) and **void** set(IndexType index, ItemType item).

> This also works for multiple indices, such as obj[index1, index2], in which the signatures contain additional parameters for the supported number of indices.

> **Slicing**: Slicing a subsequence out of a sequence is supported by mapping obj[start:end] to Type slice(**long** start, **long** end).

> **Containment**: The aforementioned in operator works with every type that implements bool contains(Type item).

> **String Template Support**: Types that implement string to_string() can be used in string templates.

Iteration: The foreach/in loop, which will be discussed in the next section, can be applied to every type that supports the method IteratorType iterator()–a type that must provide certain methods to support iteration, that is, next_value() or next() and get().

Control Flow

Within a scope, the control flow runs line by line from the top to the bottom. To manipulate the control flow, Vala supports *conditional clauses, loops*, and function/method *calls*.

Conditional Clauses

if/else The **if/else** clause executes a block, depending on a condition. Multiple clauses can be concatenated, if necessary:

```
1  if ( a > 0 )
2  {
3      return a;
4  }
5  else
6  {
7      return -a;
8  }
```

Switch The **switch** statement can be used as a shorthand for multiple concatenated **if** clauses, as it runs at most one section of code:

```
1  string value;
2
```

```
3    switch ( x ):
4    {
5        case 1:
6            value = "One";
7            break;
8
9        case 2:
10            value = "Two";
11            break;
12
13        default:
14            value = "Many";
15            break;
16   }
```

While traditionally, **switch** statements only apply to numeric values, in Vala, they can also work with strings. In contrast to C, every case statement also defines an implicit code block, that is, you don't need curly braces for defining a variable in a **case**. Also, Vala only supports the *fall-through* between cases for empty cases. In order to ensure this, each non-empty case must end with a **break**, **return,** or **throw** statement.

Loops

Vala supports four kind of loops, *while, do/while, for,* and *foreach/in*:

While: while (condition){ block } tests the given condition, and if it is valid, the block will be executed. Afterward, it starts the next iteration.

do/while: do { block } **while** (condition) executes the block, afterward evaluating the condition. If it is still valid, it starts the next iteration.

For: for (initializer; condition; afterthought){ block } is the classic **for** loop. The initializer is only called on the first run. On every run, the condition is evaluated, and then, if true, the block gets executed. Before launching the next run, the afterthought is performed.

foreach/in: foreach (type element in sequence) { block } is a variant of the **for** loop that on every run assigns the *next* element of the sequence and performs the block. This loop works for arrays and other *iterable* collections.[5]

Similarly to other programming languages, all these loop-styles are semantically equivalent, which one to prefer is merely a matter of taste—here is an example for every style:

```
1   var sequence = new string[] { "Hello", "This", "Is", "An",
    "Example" };
2
3   // while
4   var i = 0;
5   while ( i < sequence.length )
6   {
7       print( sequence[i++] );
8   }
9   // do/while
10  var j = 0;
11  do
```

---

[5]Unfortunately, the current version of the Vala compiler does not allow to iterate through strings with the foreach loop.

```
12    {
13        print( sequence[j++] );
14    }
15    while ( j < sequence.length );
16    // for
17    for ( int k = 0; k < sequence.length; ++k )
18    {
19        print( sequence[k] );
20    }
21    // foreach/in
22    foreach ( string element in sequence )
23    {
24        print( element );
25    }
```

Apart from making sure that the boolean condition evaluates to **false**, there are four ways to exit every kind of loop:

1. A **break** will exit the loop and continue execution after the block.

2. A **return** will exit the function or method context, thus leaving the loop as well.

3. A **throw** will exit the function or method context with an error condition, hence leaving the loop as well.

4. Exiting the process with a crash, or by calling the POSIX exit function, immediately exits the loop as well (of course).

Calls

A function or method call is carried out with standard brackets (),
optionally including arguments to pass from the caller to the callee. It
leaves the current execution context and returns at most one result:

```
1   foo();
2   x = bar();
3   y = baz( 10 )
```

There is no limit for the number of arguments you can pass into
a function. Since Vala does not support keyword arguments, it is
recommended to not use more than just a few, for clarity. If you need a
lot of parameters, consider passing a structure or an instance of a class
instead.

In contrast to many other programming languages, Vala does not
differentiate between functions that appear on global scope or in entities,
such as namespaces, structures, or classes—they are always named
methods. For the remainder of this book, we're following this notion.

Methods

Vala supports two kinds of method definitions, *named methods* and
anonymous methods.

Named Methods

Although we have already seen quite a few method definitions, there are
some additional concepts worth mentioning. For a better understanding
of these concepts though, we need to introduce a more general syntax for a
method definition.

In Vala, a method definition consists of seven parts with four of them being optional (indicated with brackets [...]):

```
1   [access-modifier] return-type
2   method-name ( [parameter-list] ) [throws error-list ]
3   [method-contracts]
4   {
5       code
6   }
```

Access Modifier: The access modifier controls "who" is allowed to access the method. We will discuss this in the context of object-oriented programming.

Return Type: The type of the value the method is returning. **void** denotes the absence of a return value.

Method Name: This is an identifier adhering to the rules presented earlier in this chapter. Method names can be relative to the current scope or fully qualified.

Parameter List: The list of parameters the method expects. Until now we have only passed parameters "into" methods, which is why we have declared every parameter with a type and an identifier (e.g., **int** foo). On top of that, Vala supports a *direction modifier* that modifies how parameters are passed when invoking a method. We will discuss this in Section 3.7.

Error List: As part of Vala's *structured error handling*, every method can **throw** a number of error types. This will be discussed in Section 3.8.

Method Contracts: Vala also supports a simple form of *contract-based programming*; hence every method can have a list of contracts it adheres to. Contract-based programming is briefly discussed in Section 3.9.

In Vala, every method can only be declared once per scope—there is no *method overloading*, that is, defining multiple methods with the same name but differing parameters (likewise for method contracts or error lists).

Vala allows methods to have *placeholder* arguments (sometimes also called *default values*):

```
1   void function( int x = 10 )
2   {
3       return x * 2;
4   }
5
6   var a = function( 42 ); // => 84
7   var b = function(); // => 20
```

If a caller does not supply the value for a parameter, the default value is used. Note that in order to avoid ambiguity, once a placeholder argument occurs in a parameter list, all following parameters need to have placeholder arguments as well:

```
1   void valid( int a, int b = 10, int c = 20 ); // ok
2   void invalid( int a = 10, int b ); // syntax error
```

Anonymous Methods

In addition to named methods, Vala also allows *anonymous methods*, also called *lambda expressions*. These are especially useful when calling a method that takes a delegate parameter without the need for a dedicated function—perhaps because it would never be called from somewhere else.

Anonymous methods are defined using the => operator, with the left-hand side being the parameter list and the right-hand side the code block the parameters get passed into. The following code shows how to assign an anonymous method to a delegate and how to pass it as a parameter:

```
1   delegate void VoidFuncTakingAnInt( int a );
2
3   VoidFuncTakingAnInt function = ( a ) => {
4       stdout.printf( "a = %d", a );
```

```
 5    };
 6
 7    public void methodTakingADelegate( VoidFuncTakingAnInt func )
 8    {
 9        // ...
10    }
11
12    public void someMethod()
13    {
14        methodTakingADelegate( ( a ) => {
15            stdout.printf( "a = %d", a );
16        } );
17    }
```

Note that there is no need to specify types in the parameter list, as they are already specified in the delegate declaration.

Closures

Closures are a generalized and more powerful form of anonymous methods. Closures can access local variables from the outer scope. Enhancing the previous example:

```
1    public void someMethod()
2    {
3        var x = 42;
4
5        methodTakingADelegate( ( a ) => {
6            stdout.printf( "a = %d", a );
7            x = a;
8        } );
9    }
```

Attributes

Attributes in Vala are a way to associate additional metadata to some of the language entities. The general syntax is [Annotation (details-list)]. You add an attribute by augmenting the declaration as follows:

```
1    [CCode (cname="the_c_name_of_this_variable")]
2    static int variable;
```

The attribute CCode is a low-level attribute that lets you influence the code generation; in this particular example, you are able to rename the resulting variable on the C level.

Most of those attributes are mainly useful for library bindings and will thus primarily appear in .vapi files. There are some exceptions though, for example, the previously mentioned [Flags] attribute that controls how an enumeration gets implemented.

Memory Management

Memory management is the term for controlling the lifetime of variables. The type system of Vala distinguishes between two categories of types, *value types* and *reference types*—these categories refer to the way instances of types behave when being assigned or passed as a parameter:

> **Value Types**: Instances of value types live as long as their enclosing scope is valid. When assigning to a new identifier or passing as a parameter to another method, they are copied.

> **Reference Types**: Instances of reference types are not copied but rather introduce a new name that is referencing the same entity. At the same time, their *reference counter* is being incremented. An instance of a reference type lives as long as its reference counter is greater than zero.

This kind of memory management is called *automatic reference counting*—in contrast to, for example, *garbage collection*, which is the way Java handles memory. A discussion of the advantages and disadvantages of automatic reference counting would go beyond the scope of this book though.

Parameter Passing

As you have seen earlier, value types and reference types have different characteristics when being passed as a parameter. While value types get copied, reference types are passed by reference (sic!). Until now pretty much all of our examples have only shown unidirectional parameter passing in the direction from the caller toward the callee. This is the default but can be changed by applying a *directional modifier* to the parameter specification—valid modifiers are *out* and *ref*:

In: The default way, in which the caller passes initialized values or references, which the caller may use. Modifications to those values will not be visible to the caller. In-parameters do not require (or allow) an additional modifier.

Out: An out-parameter does not pass data into the method; instead it can be used by the callee to return an additional value to the caller. Out-parameters are specified with the modifier out.

Ref: A ref-parameter (sometimes also called *inout*) can be used to pass data into a method and allows the callee to assign another value to it, in a way which is visible to the caller. Ref-parameters are indicated with the modifier ref.

In the following example, all three methods are doing the same thing; however they differ in the way the parameters are passed:

```
1   string concatenate1( string part1, string part2 )
2   {
3       return part1 + " " + part2;
```

```
 4   }
 5
 6   void concatenate2( string part1, string part2, out string
     part3 )
 7   {
 8       part3 = part1 + " " + part2;
 9   }
10
11   void concatenate3( string part1, ref string part2 )
12   {
13       part2 = part1 + " " + part2;
14   }
15
16   int main()
17   {
18       var s1 = concatenate1( "Hello", "World" );
19       stdout.printf( "%s\n", s1 ); // => "Hello World\n"
20
21       string s2;
22       concatenate2( "Hello", "World", out s2 );
23       stdout.printf( "%s\n", s2 ); // => "Hello World\n"
24
25       string s3 = "World";
26       concatenate3( "Hello", ref s3 );
27       stdout.printf( "%s\n", s3 ); // => "Hello World\n"
28
29       return 0;
30   }
```

Reference Types vs. Closures

Due to the nature of automatic reference counting, special care has to be taken when mixing closures and reference types, as this could lead to *reference cycles*. To break these, Vala knows the modifier weak.

Structured Error Handling

Vala supports structured error handling with constructs familiar to those found in languages such as C++, Java, or C#. Errors are identified by name and can contain a textual description. Related errors are grouped together into *error domains*. Note that Vala error domains do *not* form a class hierarchy, that is, you cannot define a generic error domain and derive a more specific error domain from it.

A method that raises one or multiple errors has to declare that with a **throws** keyword, followed by the list of applicable error domains. Consider this hypothetical implementation of a division method that raises an error, when the divisor is zero:

```
1   public int division( int dividend, int divisor ) throws
    MathError
2   {
3       if ( divisor == 0 )
4       {
5           throw new MathError.DivisionByZero( "Please don't
            do that!" );
6       }
7       return dividend / divisor;
8   }
```

To raise a concrete error, you have to instantiate the new error fully qualified with the message as construction parameter.

71

An error domain looks similar to an enumeration and is declared with the errordomain keyword:

```
1   public errordomain MathError
2   {
3       DIVISION_BY_ZERO,
4       OVERFLOW,
5       // ...
6   }
```

To handle an error, you have to wrap a code block that might raise one in either a **try**/**catch** or a **try**/**catch**/**finally** clause:

```
1   try
2   {
3       var x = division( 20, 30 );
4   }
5   catch ( MathError e )
6   {
7       // this block gets called when an error has occured
8   }
9   finally // the finally part is optional
10  {
11      // this block is getting called in every case
12  }
```

Multiple **catch** blocks can be used, if you want to handle different error domains individually. You can add a generic **catch** block, if you are not interested in the actual error domain but rather want to handle all error conditions in one block. It is also possible to only catch a specific error out of an error domain, that is, **catch** (MathError.OVERFLOW e){ ... }.

Note   In Vala, structured error handling should be reserved for handling recoverable run-time errors. For non-recoverable conditions, *method contracts* might be an alternative.

Method Contracts

Vala has basic support for contract-based programming. Every method can specify a boolean expression that it requires to be true before the control flow enters the code block. This boolean expression is checked at runtime, and, if it evaluates to **false**, a critical warning is emitted that usually leads to program termination.

With this, we can rewrite our last example that raised an error to signalize an invalid parameter, into the following:

```
1   public int division( int dividend, int divisor ) requires
    ( divisor != 0 )
2   {
3     return dividend / divisor;
4   }
5
6   void main()
7   {
8     var x = division( 10, 5 ); // ok
9     var y = division( 20, 0 ); // CRITICAL **: division:
      assertion ' divisor != 0' failed
10  }
```

Likewise, every method can specify a boolean expression that it ensures to be **true**, after the code block has ended:

```
1    public int abs( int value ) ensures ( result >= 0 )
2    {
3        return value > 0 ? value : -value;
4    }
```

The parameter result is a special placeholder for the return value.

For non-recoverable error conditions, contract-based programming is an alternative to structured error handling.

Summary

This chapter has presented the syntax and semantics of the majority of Vala's language constructs. By now you should be able to write many programs using the basic types with their operators, as well as handle strings, arrays, and compound types, such as structures and classes. We have also introduced Vala's memory management, structured error handling, and method contracts.

CHAPTER 4

Object-Oriented Programming

> *Curiously enough, the only thing that went through the mind of the bowl of petunias as it fell was 'Oh no, not again.' Many people have speculated that if we knew exactly why the bowl of petunias had thought that we would know a lot more about the nature of the Universe than we do now.*
>
> —Douglas Adams, The Hitchhiker's Guide to the Galaxy

This chapter goes into the details of object-oriented programming, which is the central programming paradigm of Vala, including classes, interfaces, polymorphism, and the signal mechanism for the loose binding of components.

Concepts

Object-oriented programming is a software architectural approach which originated in the 1960s. It was invented when it became evident that the increasing complexity of software systems required higher abstraction levels than previously available.

© Michael Lauer 2019
M. Lauer, *Introducing Vala Programming*, https://doi.org/10.1007/978-1-4842-5380-9_4

This is not supposed to be an introduction into object-oriented programming (OOP)—OOP is a topic for a whole book on its own—but rather a quick recall of the core concepts to get you up to speed with the terminology:

Objects: The basic idea is to view a program as a set of *objects* that combine state and behavior. Objects solve an algorithmic problem by communicating with each other.

Class: A class models an entity in the "real world," sometimes also called the *problem domain*. The class of an object defines its specifics by the means of member variables (which encapsulate state) and methods (which encapsulate behavior).

Instance: An instance is the run-time representation of an object. Two different instances of a class share the same behavior (since they belong to the same class) but may have different state (as represented by the values of their member variables). The creation of an instance is called *instantiation*. The terms instance and object are often used interchangeably.

Member Variables: Member variables encapsulate the state of an object, that is, its properties. In order to facilitate the data-hiding concept, member variables should usually be private. All mutation should be done through the behavior of the class itself.

Methods: Object communication is based on method calls. A method is pretty much like a function living in the scope of a class having access to the member variables of the current instance.

Inheritance: A class can inherit behavior from another class, called superclass. Class hierarchies may be used to model relationships that apply in the problem domain.

Polymorphism: A language supports polymorphism, when resolving a method call does not depend on the *static* type of an object, but rather its *dynamic* type—thus moving the resolve process from compile time to run-time.

Abstract Class: Adding a method without a definition (i.e., lacking a code block) to a class makes this an abstract class. In a class hierarchy, abstract classes can be used to specify a common interface with the subclasses defining the actual implementation. Objects of abstract classes cannot be instantiated.

Interface: An interface is a collection of method declarations which define an API contract for classes that inherit this interface.

Let's see how these concepts are implemented in Vala.

Classes

Visibility

The previous chapter has already introduced the access modifiers **public** and **private**. In the context of object-oriented programming, Vala allows for an even more fine-grained restriction of the visibility with the four access modifiers **private**, internal, **protected**, and **public**:

Private: Access is limited to the current **class** or struct defined by the enclosing scope.

Internal: Access is limited to the current *package*—this is merely useful when creating a library.

Protected: Access is limited to the current **class** and all of its subclasses.

Public: No access restrictions applied.

Inheritance

Vala supports single inheritance: A **class** can inherit from zero or one superclasses plus any number of **interface**s.

GLib.Object As mentioned, when defining a new class, Vala does not require inheriting from a superclass. It also doesn't implicitly add any superclasses to a newly defined class. Some features though are only available if you derive your class from GLib.Object.[1]

A class that does not derive (either directly or through a superclass) from GLib.Object is called *pure*, *plain*, or *lightweight*. In this book, we will use the term "plain."

Construction

The constructor is the first code that runs when a new instance is being created with operator **new**. While constructors are optional, they're recommended for initializing member variables or acquiring resources. There are four kinds of constructors in Vala: *Default* constructor, *Named* constructor, *Construction Block*, and *Static Construction Block*:

Default Constructor: The default constructor has the same name as its class. It does not return any values (specifying **void** is forbidden, since it already "returns" the instance) but may accept a parameter list. It can **throw** errors. Specifying pre- and postconditions is allowed (the special parameter result makes no sense in a constructor context and is hence forbidden).

Named Constructor: Since Vala does not support method overloading, multiple named constructors are allowed in addition to the one-and-only default constructor. Apart from the naming, named constructors must follow the same rules as default constructors.

---

[1]This boils down to the difference of glib's *static* and *fundamental* type concept. Classes derived from GLib.Object are registered with g_type_register_static(), others are registered with g_type_register_fundamental().

Construction Block: Only available for classes derived from GLib. Object, construction blocks run right after registering the class with the underlying glib type system. They can be used as an alternative or in addition to the other constructors. Construction blocks do not accept any parameters and do not support pre- or postconditions.

Static Construction Block: Sometimes it is necessary to perform additional initialization the first time an instance of a class is created. Static construction blocks are also supported for plain classes.

The following code listing shows all valid kinds of constructors in action:

```
1   class Class : Object
2   {
3       static construct
4       {
5           stdout.printf( "static construction block\n" );
6       }
7
8       public Class()
9       {
10          stdout.printf( "default constructor\n" );
11      }
12
13      public Class.with_param( int x )
14      {
15          stdout.printf( "named constructor\n" );
16      }
17
18      construct
19      {
20          stdout.printf( "construct block\n" );
21      }
22  }
23
```

```
24   void main()
25   {
26       var c = new Class();
27       var d = new Class();
28       var e = new Class.with_param( 10 );
29   }
```

Running this leads to the following sequence of messages:

```
1   static construction block
2   construct block
3   default constructor
4   construct block
5   default constructor
6   construct block
7   named constructor
```

We can observe that the static construction block runs first (but only once), then the per-instance construct block, and after that the default constructor. The order of named and default constructors can change, if *chaining* (see the following) is used.

Chaining: There are two ways of chaining constructors, *chaining up* to the superclass and *crosschaining* to another, more generic, constructor in the same class:

Chaining Up: Default constructors not taking any parameters will automatically chain up to the superclass. If your default constructor is parametrized with at least one parameter that does not contain a default argument, then this automatism will no longer work. In that case you are required to chain up explicitly with the base keyword:

```
1   class Base
2   {
3       public Base( int x )
```

```
4        {
5              stdout.printf( "base constructor\n" );
6        }
7    }
8
9    class Class : Base
10   {
11       public Class()
12       {
13             stdout.printf( "default constructor\n" );
14             base( 10 ); // if this one missing, you will get:
15             // "error: unable to chain up to base constructor
                 requiring arguments"
16       }
17   }
18
19   void main()
20   {
21       var c = new Class();
22   }
```

Crosschaining: Multiple named constructors are often helpful when instances can be created with different sets of input parameters. Usually, you will define the generic constructor and call it from the more specific constructors. Crosschaining can be done using the **this** keyword:

```
1    public class Point : Object
2    {
3        public double x;
4        public double y;
5
6        public Point( double x, double y )
```

```
7      {
8          this.x = x;
9          this.y = y;
10     }
11
12     public Point.rectangular( double x, double y )
13     {
14         this( x, y );
15     }
16
17     public Point.polar( double radius, double angle )
18     {
19         this.rectangular( radius * Math.cos(angle),
           radius * Math.sin(angle) );
20     }
21 }
22
23 void main()
24 {
25     var p1 = new Point.rectangular( 5.7, 1.2 );
26     var p2 = new Point.polar( 5.7, 1.2 );
27 }
```

Destruction

If you want to execute a block of code before an instance gets deallocated (as a consequence of the last reference being removed), you can define a destructor adhering to the following rules:

- It has to have the same name as the class prepended by a tilde (~).

- No access modifier can be given, since it is not explicitly callable (the run-time calls it implicitly).

- It is not allowed to return or take any parameters.

- It cannot throw errors or support pre- or postconditions.

```
1   public class Destructor
2   {
3       ~Destructor()
4       {
5           stdout.printf( "destructor" );
6       }
7   }
```

Multiple destructors are not possible.

Member Variables

Member variables in classes define state. An object can contain any number of member variables. Member variables can have an optional access modifier and an optional initial value. If you don't specify the initial value, the member variable gets initialized with 0 (or **null**, respectively). By default, member variables are *instance members*, that is, their value is associated to an actual instance of the class:

```
1    public class MyClass
2    {
3        private int x;
4        protected int y = 10;
5        public int z;
6    }
7
8    void main()
9    {
10       var c = new MyClass();
```

83

```
11        c.x = 10; // error: Access to private member
                        `MyClass.x' denied.
12        c.z = 20; // ok
13    }
```

It is also possible to declare *class-wide* member variables. For this you need to use the **static** modifier and a fully qualified reference (with the class name as the prefix):

```
1    public class MyClass
2    {
3        public static int x;
4    }
5
6    void main()
7    {
8        MyClass.x = 10; // ok
9    }
```

You can also refer to a static member variable by using an instance. Change the main() function from the preceding code to

```
1    void main()
2    {
3        MyClass.x = 10; // ok
4
5        var obj1 = new MyClass();
6        print( "obj1.x = %d\n", obj1.x ); // => "obj1.x = 10"
7        var obj2 = new MyClass();
8        print( "obj2.x = %d\n", obj2.x ); // => "obj2.x = 10"
9    }
```

This form is not advisable though, since it may lead to confusion: It's not clear anymore that you are referring to a class-wide member variable.

Class Constants

If you need a constant value in the scope of a class, you can define it as **const**. This looks very similar to a constant value defined in a namespace:

```
1   public class MyClass
2   {
3       public const int y = 42;
4   }
```

In contrast to constants in namespaces, access modifiers are supported.

Enumerations

Enumerations contained in the scope of a class behave identically to enumerations in namespaces.

Note   The current version of the Vala compiler (0.46 at the time of writing) ignores the access modifiers given to an enumeration in the class scope—it is always treated as **public**.

Methods

Methods in classes define behavior. An object can contain any number of methods. As shown in the previous chapter, methods can have a complex definition, including access modifiers, parameter lists, error, and contract specifications. Methods also require a code block as body.

```
1   public class MyClass
2   {
3       public int callme()
```

```
4        {
5            return 42;
6        }
7    }
8
9    void main()
10   {
11       var c = new MyClass();
12       var x = c.callme();
13   }
```

Similar to member variables, there is a way to define class-wide methods, also called *class methods*, using the **static** modifier:

```
1    public class MyClass
2    {
3        public static int callme()
4        {
5            return 42;
6        }
7    }
8
9    void main()
10   {
11       var x = MyClass.callme();
12   }
```

Identically to the preceding code, while you *can* also call a static class-wide method on an instance, note that—in order to prevent confusion—it is not advisable. The following code triggers the compiler warning "Access to static member MyClass.callme with an instance reference":

```
1   void main()
2   {
3       var obj = new MyClass();
4       var x = obj.callme(); // triggers a compiler warning
5   }
```

Note   Calling a class method will *not* create a new instance of a class; hence it will not trigger a static construction block.

Abstract Classes

Vala supports the notion of *abstract classes*, that is, classes that can't be instantiated. Only abstract classes can contain *abstract methods* (methods without a code block as body). To declare an abstract class, use the modifier **abstract**:

```
1   public abstract class AbstractBaseClass
2   {
3       public abstract void doit();
4   }
```

For any non-abstract class that inherits from an abstract class, you must implement all abstract methods. Otherwise you will get a compiler error:

```
1   error: `ConcreteClass' does not implement abstract method `
    AbstractBaseClass.doit'
```

To indicate that you are implementing an abstract method, use the modifier override:

```
1  public abstract class AbstractBaseClass
2  {
3      public abstract void doit();
4  }
5
6  public class ConcreteClass : AbstractBaseClass
7  {
8      public override void doit()
9      {
10         // ...
11     }
12 }
13
14 void main()
15 {
16     var c = new ConcreteClass();
17 }
```

Polymorphism

Vala supports polymorphism by the means of *virtual* methods. Consider the following example where the called method is depending on the static type of the variable:

```
1  class One
2  {
3      public void doit()
4      {
5          stdout.printf( "One does it!\n" );
6      }
```

```
 7    }
 8
 9    class Two : One
10    {
11        public void doit()
12        {
13            stdout.printf( "Two does it!\n" );
14        }
15    }
16
17    void main()
18    {
19        One one = new One(); // static type == dynamic type
20        one.doit();
21
22        Two two = new Two(); // static type == dynamic type
23        two.doit();
24
25        One what = new Two(); // static type != dynamic type
26        what.doit();
27    }
```

Running this will produce the following output:

```
1    One does it!
2    Two does it!
3    One does it!
```

Although the actual (dynamic) type of the what variable is Two, the compiler calls the method in the superclass; thus it behaves like if it was of type One.[2]

The compiler resolves the actual method to call at compile time. When working with class hierarchies, this behavior is often undesirable (the value of this might not fully come across in this simple example, but consider *factory methods* or *class clusters*, where you don't know what (sub-)type is actually returned by a method).

Let's change the class definitions from the previous example using the modifiers virtual and override like that:

```
1   class One
2   {
3        public virtual void doit()
4        {
5            stdout.printf( "One does it!\n" );
6        }
7   }
8
9   class Two : One
10  {
11       public override void doit()
12       {
13           stdout.printf( "Two does it!\n" );
14       }
15  }
16
```

---

[2]An indicator of an upcoming problem is the triggered compiler warning "warning: Two.doit hides inherited method One.doit. Use the **new** keyword if hiding was intentional." Following this advice won't solve the mentioned problem though.

```
17   void main()
18   {
19       One one = new One(); // static type == dynamic type
20       one.doit();
21
22       Two two = new Two(); // static type == dynamic type
23       two.doit();
24
25       One what = new Two(); // static type != dynamic type
26       what.doit();
27   }
```

If we run it now, we get the expected behavior:

```
1   One does it!
2   Two does it!
3   Two does it!
```

Chaining Up: Sometimes you want to *extend* the implementation of a (virtual) method rather than completely replacing it; thus you need a way to chain up to the superclass. This can be done using the keyword base, which—in every method of a class that has a superclass—refers to the superclass' part of the current instance:

```
1   public void doit()
2   {
3       stdout.printf( "Two does it!\n" );
4       base.doit();
5   }
```

Signals

Signals are a device for the loose coupling of unidirectional method calls. A signal represents an event, which other parts of the code can subscribe to and get notified when it gets triggered (or *emitted*, which is the common technical term for it). Consider the following example program:

```
1    public class Test : Object
2    {
3        int counter;
4
5        public signal void ring( int a );
6
7        public void trigger()
8        {
9            ring( counter++ );
10       }
11   }
12
13   public void ringHandler( Test source, int a )
14   {
15       stdout.printf( "ringHandler called: %d\n", a );
16   }
17
18   void main()
19   {
20       var t = new Test();
21
22       t.ring.connect( ringHandler );
23
24       t.ring.connect( ( source, a ) => {
25           stdout.printf( "%d\n", a );
```

```
26        });
27
28        t.trigger();
29   }
```

Signals belong to the interface of a class. The declaration looks similar to a method without a body:

```
1    public signal void ring( int a );
```

To add a signal handler (sometimes also called *listener*) to a `signal`, you call the `connect` method on the `signal`, either with a `delegate` or an anonymous method with a matching signature:

```
1    t.ring.connect( ( source, a ) => {
2        stdout.printf( "%d\n", a );
3    });
```

Signals are emitted by calling them like a method:

```
1    ring( counter++ );
```

The listener has to have a compatible signature,[3] for example, the parameter list as declared by the signal, plus the *source* (which is an instance of the class the signal belongs to) inserted as the first parameter:

```
1    public void ringHandler( Test source, int a ) { ... }
```

---

[3]If you're not interested in the actual sender, you can leave out this parameter in the signal handler. You may also omit any number of trailing parameters. You can even connect signal handlers not taking any parameters, independent of the actual signal signature.

Note   The current version of the compiler provides no access control for signals. They have to be **public** and everyone can `connect` to a signal as well as trigger its emission.

Disconnecting There are two ways for disconnecting an event handler from a signal:

- Either call the `disconnect` method on the signal with the same parameter you gave to the `connect` method, or

- Save the `ulong` return parameter (called *signal handler id*) from `connect`, and use it in your call to `disconnect`.

Properties

The direct access to member variables is often undesirable (data hiding is a core goal when using object-orientation). To access the values of private member variables, special *getter* and *setter* methods are created (also called *accessors*).

Vala provides a special syntax for such accessors, called *properties*. A property is the combination of a member variable with associated accessor methods for reading and/or writing. The keyword `get` introduces the getter; the clause `set` defines the setter:

```
1   public class Person
2   {
3       private string _name = "No Name";
4
5       public string name {
6           get { return _name; }
7           set { _name = value; }
8       }
```

```
 9   }
10
11   void main()
12   {
13       var p = new Person();
14       p.name = "Dr. med. Wurst"; // invokes the setter
15       stdout.printf( "The person's name is: %s\n", p.name );
         // invokes the getter
16   }
```

The getter method has to return a value of the properties' specified type. In the case of the setter method, the keyword value is the placeholder for the input parameter. Since these accessor methods contain standard code blocks, they have the same possibilities as every other method— including variable access and calling any other methods.

If, as outlined in the following example, the accessor methods only proxy the access to a **private** member variable, you can simplify the definition of a property even more:

```
1   public class Person
2   {
3       public string name {
4           get;
5           set;
6           default = "No Name";
7       }
8   }
```

This automatically creates a corresponding private member variable *backing* the property and implements the necessary accessor methods. The optional **default** clause is helpful if you need an initial value for the property.

Notifications Another handy feature of properties is the built-in support for *notifications*: Every class inherited by GLib.Object has a signal called notify. This signal is emitted whenever a change of any property occurs. You can connect a listener and handle the notification as follows:

```
1   obj.notify.connect( (source, property) => {
2       stdout.printf( "Property '%s' has changed!\n",
        property.name );
3   });
```

If you are only interested in a specific property, you can use the subscription operator [ ] to connect the handler to only one property:

```
1   obj.notify["name"].connect( source, property ) => {
2       stdout.printf( "Name property has changed!\n" );
3   };
```

Note   Due to the underlying implementation in glib, when referring to a specific property, you need to use the string representation of the property name, in which underscores (_) are replaced by dashes (-). A property this_is_a_property would then become "this-is-a-property".

Interfaces

Interfaces in Vala are similar to abstract classes. While a class can only have one superclass though, it is possible to add multiple interfaces as prerequisites. An interface can also have one or multiple other interfaces as prerequisites. Consequently, interfaces do not support member variables.

Interfaces can contain abstract methods or methods with an implementation, the latter being treated as virtual methods. Interfaces also support signals and properties.

OOP and the Type System

As mentioned before, in the context of Vala's type system, classes (and interfaces) are reference types. They're *registered* with the type system at run-time which allows for some special capabilities:

Run-Time Type Information (RTTI)

While it is good OOP practice not to rely on the actual type of an object (i.e., better use polymorphism rather than type checks), it may sometimes be necessary to do so. The is operator allows you to check whether an object is an instance of a certain type:

```
1   public interface SomeInterface {}
2   public abstract class AbstractBaseClass {}
3   public class ConcreteClass : AbstractBaseClass,
    SomeInterface {}
4   public class SomeClass {}
5
6   void main()
7   {
8       var x = new ConcreteClass();
9       bool b = x is SomeInterface;     // => true
10      bool c = x is ConcreteClass;     // => true
11      bool d = x is AbstractBaseClass; // => true
12      bool e = x is SomeClass;         // => false
13  }
```

In addition to that, every instance of a class inherited from GLib. Object has access to the get_type () method which returns an object representing the type of that instance:

```
1   public class Cat : Object {}
2
3   void main()
4   {
5       var cat = new Cat();
6       Type aType = cat.get_type();
7       string aName = aType.name(); => "Cat"
8   }
```

While printing the type name is not particularly useful, the beauty of RTTI lies in the ability to create new instances based on that type. Use the class method Object.new():

```
1   public class Cat : Object {}
2
3   void main()
4   {
5       var cat = new Cat(); // Cat
6       Type aType = cat.get_type();
7       var cat2 = Object.new( aType ); // Another cat
8       var cat3 = Object.new( typeof( Cat ) ); // Triplets!
9   }
```

Note that you can also apply the typeof() operator on a class name: This returns the type object of a class or an interface.

Dynamic Type Casting

Dynamic type casting with operator as is an alternative to using the is operator. This operator will check the dynamic type of the right-hand side at run-time and returns either the argument itself (if the type matches) or **null** (if it doesn't):

```
1    public class Animal {}
2    public class Cat : Animal {}
3    public class Dog : Animal {}
4
5    void main()
6    {
7        var cat = new Cat();
8        var dog = new Dog();
9
10       Animal catAnimal = cat; // => nothing to do, upcast
11       Cat stillACat = catAnimal as Cat; // => ok, valid
          downcast
12       Dog dogAnimal = cat as Dog; // => null, invalid downcast
13       Dog d2 = (Dog) cat; // => undefined, runtime warning
14   }
```

Warning   If you're using the static type cast syntax as explained in static type casting, Vala will insert a *checked* dynamic cast that does *not* result in **null** but will emit a glib warning at run-time.[4]

---

[4]Unfortunately, just emitting a warning here is not quite helpful, since (a) you can't catch the warning and (b) the assignment still "works." It would have been better to set the variable to **null**, if the dynamic type cast fails.

Generics

Generic programming is an approach for writing algorithms that operate on values independent of their actual type. Vala provides support for *generic classes, generic structures,* and *generic interfaces.* The generic type specification is appended in angle brackets (< and >) right after the **class**/struct /**interface** name. Within the scope, you can refer to the generic type by name. Here is an example for a managed array list operating on elements of type T:

```
1   interface List<T>
2   {
3       public abstract void add( T element ); // adds an
        element at the end
4       public abstract T peek(); // returns the last element
5       public abstract void remove(); // removes the last
        element
6   }
```

Let's create a concrete class that implements this interface with a Vala array:

```
1   class MyList<T> : List<T>
2   {
3       T[] array;
4
5       public void add( T element )
6       {
7           array += element;
8       }
9
```

```
10        public T peek()
11        {
12            return array[array.length - 1];
13        }
14
15        public void remove()
16        {
17            array[array.length - 1] = null; // omitting this
              will leak memory
18            array.resize( array.length - 1 );
19        }
20  }
```

Now let's put this to the test with a List of strings:

```
1   void main()
2   {
3       var q = new MyList<string>();
4       q.add( "first string\n" );
5       q.add( "second string\n" );
6       stdout.printf( "%s", q.peek() );
7       q.remove();
8       stdout.printf( "%s", q.peek() );
9   }
```

Running this snippet leads to the expected output:

```
1   second string
2   first string
```

Classes vs. Structures

Since Vala structures can contain methods, sometimes classes might not be necessary, for example, when you only want to provide some helper methods that operate on a bunch of grouped data. Be aware though that structures are stack allocated (hence copied when on assignment), while classes are allocated on the heap.

In fact, the decision when to use a class or a structure is even more complicated: Apart from plain classes and classes derived from GLib. Object, there is a third type of class that hasn't been mentioned yet: *compact class*.

Compact classes are not registered with the underlying glib type system and do not support reference counting or private fields. You can use unmanaged properties though, since these are just syntactic sugar for standard methods. Since Vala 0.40, compact classes can even support virtual and abstract methods. Compact classes need less memory and are instantiated much faster than plain classes. Since they are also reference-based, they might be an alternative to using structs.

You declare a compact class by using the code attribute Compact:

```
1   [Compact]
2   public class Example
3   {
4       public void foo()
5       {
6           stdout.printf( "I'm a compact class!\n" );
7       }
8   }
9
```

```
10   void main()
11   {
12       var example = new Example();
13       example.foo(); // => "I'm a compact class"
14   }
```

Summary

We have presented the core concepts of object-oriented programming as well as their implementation in Vala. The signal mechanism is a way to loosely couple components. Use interfaces to factor out common behavior. Generics can be helpful to formulate algorithms that work with all kinds of types.

CHAPTER 5

Networking

"But the plans were on display..."

"On display? I eventually had to go down to the cellar to find them."

"That's the display department."

"With a flashlight."

"Ah, well, the lights had probably gone."

"So had the stairs."

"But look, you found the notice, didn't you?"

"Yes," said Arthur, "yes I did. It was on display in the bottom of a locked filing cabinet stuck in a disused lavatory with a sign on the door saying 'Beware of the Leopard'."

—Douglas Adams, The Hitchhiker's Guide to the Galaxy

This chapter covers network programming with Vala. We're introducing the low-level way using POSIX sockets first and then advance to using GIO. Since most web services these days are talking JSON, we're also going to introducing this. Last but not least, we will present the GNOME HTTP networking library libsoup.

© Michael Lauer 2019
M. Lauer, *Introducing Vala Programming*, https://doi.org/10.1007/978-1-4842-5380-9_5

Sockets

Sockets abstract the communication between hosts interconnected by the means of a local network and/or the Internet. Sockets support both the *packet-oriented* (UDP) and *stream-oriented* (TCP) protocols.[1]

Sockets as an API have been introduced as part of the Berkeley Unix Distribution (4.2BSD) and have been subsequently standardized as part of POSIX.

Sockets in posix.vapi

The following parts of the Socket API are supported by Vala:

socket() creates a new socket of a certain socket type, identified by an integer number, and allocates system resources to it.

bind() is typically used on the server side, and associates a socket with a socket address structure, that is, a specified local port number and IP address.

listen() is used on the server side, and causes a bound TCP socket to enter listening state.

connect() is used on the client side, and assigns a free local port number to a socket. In the case of a TCP socket, it causes an attempt to establish a new TCP connection.

accept() is used on the server side. It accepts an attempt from the client to create a new TCP connection and creates a new socket associated with the socket address pair of this connection.

send() or write() and recv()/read() are used for sending and receiving data *to* or *from* a remote socket.

close() causes the system to release resources allocated to a socket. In the case of TCP, the connection is terminated.

---

[1]In fact they support much more, e.g., SCTP, DCCP, IPPROTO_RAW, ICMP. TCP and UDP are the most common ones though.

`gethostbyname()` and `gethostbyaddr()` are used to resolve hostnames and addresses (IPv4 only).

`select()` is used to wait for a number of sockets until one (or more) of them changes their state (ready to read, ready to write, error).

`poll()` is used to check the state of a set of sockets (ready to read, ready to write, error).

`getsockopt()` is used to retrieve the current value of a particular option for the specified socket.

`setsockopt()` is used to set a particular option for the specified socket.

As an example, we learn how to gather the current date and time from a time server using the *Network Time Protocol (NTP)*. We will write code that sends a well-formatted NTP packet to the server, receives an answer, and parses it to display the server's time on the console.[2]

Example: NTP Client

Originating in 1985, NTP is one of the oldest Internet protocols. It is a connectionless protocol for synchronizing clocks. At the time of writing, the latest published version was NTP v3.

As usual with network protocols, a major part of the specification is the description of the packet data format. For NTP, this is a 48-byte payload, which we can define in Vala using the following `struct`:

```
1    struct NtpPacket
2    {
3        uint8 li_vn_mode;
4        uint8 stratum;
5        uint8 poll;
6        uint8 precision;
```

---

[2]Of course, we could have used something like `libntp` to handle all the nitty and gritty low-level details, but that would be "cheating."

```
7          uint32 rootDelay;
8          uint32 rootDispersion;
9          uint32 refId;
10         uint32 refTm_s;
11         uint32 refTm_f;
12         uint32 origTm_s;
13         uint32 origTm_f;
14         uint32 rxTm_s;
15         uint32 rxTm_f;
16         uint32 txTm_s;
17         uint32 txTm_f;
18  }
```

When implementing network protocols, it is important to rely on fixed-width integer types; hence we are using uint8 and uint32 here. Luckily, we will only have to deal with a handful of those fields, in particular li_vn_mode, which we have to set to 0x1b in order to get a well-formatted NTPv3 request packet:

```
1   var packet = NtpPacket();
2   assert( sizeof( NtpPacket ) == 48 );
3   packet.li_vn_mode = 0x1b;
```

Initially, we instantiate the structure, make sure that it has the expected size, and set the necessary fields to make it a well-formatted NTPv3 request packet.

Now that we have constructed the NTP packet structure, we need to define the recipient. For the address, we can use the hostname and a port number of any publicly available NTP server:

```
1   const string hostname = "pool.ntp.org";
2   const uint16 portno = 123; // NTP
```

As hostname we're using `pool.ntp.org`, which is a dynamic collection of time servers on the Internet. NTP servers are going to listen on port 123, which is the *well-known port number* for NTP:

```
1   unowned Posix.HostEnt server = Posix.gethostbyname
    ( hostname );
2   if ( server == null )
3   {
4   error( @"Can't resolve host $hostname: $(Posix.errno)" );
5   }
6   print( @"Found $(server.h_addr_list.length) IP address(es)
    for $hostname\n" );
```

Since lower level network protocols deal with IP addresses rather than alphanumerical hostnames, the first thing we have to do is *resolve* the server name to an IP address. POSIX defines gethostbyname(), which is a synchronous method returning an unowned[3] HostEnt structure:

```
1   var address = Posix.SockAddrIn();
2   address.sin_family = Posix.AF_INET;
3   address.sin_port = Posix.htons( portno );
4   Posix.memcpy( &address.sin_addr, server.h_addr_list[0],
    server.h_length );
5   var stringAddress = Posix.inet_ntoa( address.sin_addr );
6   print( @"Using $hostname IP address $stringAddress\n" );
```

To prepare the packet, we need to construct the socket address, which is mapped by `posix.vapi` as the structure SockAddrIn. We set the protocol family to AF_INET (which stands for TCP/IP and UDP/IP) and the port to the aforementioned port number for NTP. The IP address is copied from

---

[3]Functions defined in POSIX often return *pointers* to internal storage, which are not supposed to be released by the caller. In Vala, these functions are mapped as methods returning unowned types.

the HostEnt structure returned by gethostbyname(). Since this is a nested structure, a simple assignment is not sufficient—we have to copy the bytes by using the POSIX's memcpy(). In order to print the actual IP address, we call the POSIX function inet_ntoa(), which returns a printable string.

Note   When representing values, different CPU architectures may use different internal byte orders, most commonly referred to as *little endian* (least significant byte first) and *big endian* (most significant byte first). As long as your program works only locally and is not communicating with other computers, you can safely ignore this fact. To support a heterogenous communication network consisting of potentially unknown computers (hence using different CPU architectures), a standardized *network order* has been defined.

To make sure we're using the correct representation, POSIX defines utility functions, such as htons, htonl, ntohl, and ntohs, to convert between the architecture-specific *host order* and the generic *network order*:

```
1   var sockfd = Posix.socket( Posix.AF_INET, Posix.SOCK_DGRAM,
    Posix.IPProto.UDP );
2   if ( sockfd < 0 )
3   {
4       error( @"Can't create socket: $(Posix.errno)" );
5   }
```

In UNIX, sockets are represented as *file descriptors*. Given an address family and a protocol type, the POSIX socket() function returns such a file descriptor. Many POSIX functions return status codes (0, if everything worked correctly; a negative value, if there was an error) and set the global error number variable errno, if necessary:

```
1    var ok = Posix.connect( sockfd, address, sizeof( Posix.
     SockAddrIn ) );
2    if ( ok < 0 )
3    {
4        error( @"Can't connect: $(Posix.errno)" );
5    }
```

After a socket was created, we need to connect() to it before we can send or receive data. The POSIX connect() takes a file descriptor for a socket, the address (which we have constructed as a structure beforehand), and the length of this address structure (different types of address families may have different structures and sizes):

```
1    var written = Posix.write( sockfd, &packet,
     sizeof( NtpPacket ) );
2    if ( written < 0 )
3    {
4        error( "Can't send UDP packet: $(Posix.errno)" );
5    }
```

Now we can finally send the NTP packet with POSIX's write(), which takes three parameters: A file descriptor, the address of a buffer that contains the bytes to send, and the number of bytes to send. write() returns the number of bytes actually written (partial writes are always possible, a fact that we however ignore in this simple example). A negative return value indicates that an error occurred—in that case, we print the value of errno on the console:

```
1    var received = Posix.read( sockfd, &packet,
     sizeof( NtpPacket ) );
2    if ( received < 0 )
3    {
4        error( "Can't read from socket: $(Posix.errno)" );
5    }
```

When the buffer has successfully been sent, we use POSIX's read() to wait for an answer. read() expects a file descriptor, a buffer to write the received bytes into, and the maximum size of this buffer.

After write() returned with a nonnegative return value, the request has been successfully sent, and we no longer need the data contained in the NtpPacket structure. Thus, we may reuse it as the buffer for the answer packet. This is valid, since, according to the protocol, both the NTP request and answer packets have the same format and size.

read() returns the number of received bytes, or a negative value, if an error occurs. A proper program should check whether we actually received all 48 bytes that form the NTP packet payload (remember, fragmentation is always possible):

```
1   packet.txTm_s = Posix.ntohl( packet.txTm_s );
2   packet.txTm_f = Posix.ntohl( packet.txTm_f );
3   const uint64 NTP_TIMESTAMP_DELTA = 2208988800ull;
4   time_t txTm = ( time_t ) ( packet.txTm_s - NTP_TIMESTAMP_
    DELTA );
```

To gather the time information from the packet, we use the NTP packet fields txTm_s and txTm_f (which we have to convert into host order). The net result of all that is the current UTC time in form of POSIX's time_t:

```
1   var str = Posix.ctime( ref txTm );
2   print( @"Current UTC time is $str" );
```

Finally, we are using POSIX's ctime(), which converts a time_t into a readable string representation. Running this code produces the following output:

```
1   $ ./ntpClient-example
2   Found 4 IP address(es) for pool.ntp.org
3   Using pool.ntp.org IP address 185.210.224.85
4   Current UTC time is Tue Jan 16 17:10:22 2018
```

Note   Since we're using entities from `posix.vapi`, don't forget to include `--pkg=posix` when compiling the example.

JSON

As you have seen in the previous section, binary protocols are somewhat cumbersome to deal with, as you have to define structures on byte (or even bit) level and take extreme care that your field lengths match the specification. For a protocol as simple as NTP, this looks easy enough; however if you consider dynamic field lengths and/or nested fields, the benefits of using higher level protocols and/or data exchange formats become evident.

The *JavaScript Object Notation (JSON)* is such an exchange format. By now it has pretty much replaced XML (and SOAP) as the most popular data exchange format for web services.

The JSON syntax definition contains *basic types* and *compound types*. JSON has the following basic types:

- **STRING**: A string, formatted in double quotes: `"This is a string"`

- **NUMBER**: A number: 123, or 0.123

- **BOOLEAN: true** or **false**

- **NULL: null**

On top of that, two compound types are defined:

- **ARRAY**: An ordered sequence of values: [1, 2, 3]

- **OBJECT**: A collection of key/value pairs: { "id": 1234, "name": "Harry"}

113

For the contents of ARRAY and OBJECT, a valid value can either be a basic type or another compound type (you can nest structures as you see fit). For OBJECT, a valid key must be a STRING. Note that JSON ARRAYs do not need to be homogenous, that is, the same ARRAY can contain both a number and a string.

A valid JSON document needs to have a compound structure as the top-level value, that is, either an ARRAY or an OBJECT.

Here is an example of a valid JSON document that has been retrieved from a weather web service, providing the weather status for a given location:

```
1    {
2        "current": {
3            "cloud": 75,
4            "condition": {
5                "code": 1183,
6                "icon": "//cdn.apixu.com/weather/64x64/day/
                 296.png",
7                "text": "Light rain"
8            },
9            "feelslike_c": 8.6,
10           "feelslike_f": 47.5,
11           "humidity": 94,
12           "is_day": 1,
13           "last_updated": "2018-01-18 12:00",
14           "last_updated_epoch": 1516273229,
15           "precip_in": 0.03,
16           "precip_mm": 0.8,
17           "pressure_in": 30.2,
18           "pressure_mb": 1006.0,
19           "temp_c": 11.0,
20           "temp_f": 51.8,
21           "vis_km": 1.5,
```

```
22          "vis_miles": 0.0,
23          "wind_degree": 290,
24          "wind_dir": "WNW",
25          "wind_kph": 20.2,
26          "wind_mph": 12.5
27      },
28      "location": {
29          "country": "France",
30          "lat": 48.87,
31          "localtime": "2018-01-18 12:19",
32          "localtime_epoch": 1516274374,
33          "lon": 2.33,
34          "name": "Paris",
35          "region": "Ile-de-France",
36          "tz_id": "Europe/Paris"
37      }
38  }
```

Vala contains a binding for the library json-glib, which can be used to encode or decode JSON documents. Let's look at an example that reads this weather report from stdin and prints out a readable summary.

Example: JSON Parser

```
1   var buffer = new uint8[5000];
2   var numRead = stdin.read( buffer, 5000 );
3   var jsonString = (string)buffer;
```

A simple way to get a string from stdin is to read() it into a character buffer and then treat this as a string. read() will terminate when it encounters the EOF:

```
1   var root = Json.from_string( jsonString );
```

We parse the jsonString using the static convenience function from_string. Behind the scenes, this method creates a Json.Parser and calls load_from_data(). If the data is a well-formatted JSON document, then it returns a Json.Node representing its root node (either an array or an object). If not, an Error is raised. For production-ready code, you should wrap this in a **try/catch** block.

json-glib treats JSON documents as a tree data structure containing individual nodes. We will now navigate through this tree to extract the information we need. For our output, we want to gather the following values:

- current/condition/text contains a STRING representing a human readable summary of the weather condition.

- current/temp_c contains a NUMBER representing the measured temperature in degrees Celsius.

- current/feelslike_c contains a NUMBER representing how the measured temperature actually feels like, considering other environmental conditions:

```
1  var rootObject = root.get_object();
```

A Json.Node wraps a generic node in the JSON document tree, which can contain a value of any of the basic or compound types. In our case we know the actual type (OBJECT); hence we can directly get the Json.Object out of the root node. If we had to deal with an unknown document structure, we can use type_name() to peek into the type of value the Json.Node contains:

```
1  var currentObject = rootObject.get_object_member( "current" );
```

The method JsonObject.get_object_member(string name) reads the value for the key name and returns a Json.Object (if this member is actually an OBJECT). Here, we get the OBJECT with the current weather data:

```
1   var conditionObject = currentObject.get_object_member
    ( "condition" );
```

Similar to the preceding code, conditionObject now contains the condition OBJECT, which contains summary information of the current weather condition:

```
1   var conditionText = conditionObject.get_string_member
    ( "text" );
```

Likewise, conditionText now contains a STRING representing a human readable textual description of the weather condition:

```
1   var tempC = currentObject.get_double_member( "temp_c" );
2   var feelsLikeC = currentObject.get_double_member
    ( "feelslike_c" );
```

Next to the condition, the currentObject also contains details about the current weather data, in particular the measured temperature and the derived temperature, both being NUMBER members, represented as **double**s in Vala:

```
1   print( "Current condition is '%s' with %.1f°C, feeling
    like %.1f°C\n", conditionText, tempC, feelsLikeC );
```

Here we assemble the final string. Running this on my machine produces the following output:

```
1   $ cat report.json | vala --pkg=json-glib-1.0 jsonParser.vala
2   Current condition is 'Partly cloudy' with 11.0°C, feeling
    like 6.6°C
```

Note   Don't forget to supply the command-line argument `--pkg=json-glib-1.0`, since we are using entities defined in `json-glib-1.0.vapi`. If you get a compilation error like

```
1    jsonParser.vala.BIZ3CZ.c:10:10: fatal error: 'json-glib/
     json-glib.h' file not found
2    #include <json-glib/json-glib.h>
3             ^~~~~~~~~~~~~~~~~~~~~~~~
4    1 error generated.
5    error: cc exited with status 256
```

then the library `json-glib` has not been installed on your machine.

GIO

For higher level networking, Vala comes with a binding to gio, which is a generic input/output library based on `glib`. gio contains APIs for synchronous and asynchronous (network) transfers, the latter being especially relevant for developing graphical user interfaces. As these are typically based on event loops, non-blocking APIs are required.

As an example, we will now learn how to query a web server, specifically, a web service providing a JSON weather report similar to the one presented in the previous section.

Note   To run this example on your machine, you need to apply for an API key at `www.apixu.com` —unfortunately there are no public weather forecast services that do not require an account.

Example: HTTP Client with GIO

```
1    var host = "api.apixu.com";
2    var port = 80;
3    var key = "<apikey>";
4    var city = "Paris";
5    var query = @"/v1/current.json?key=$key&q=$city";
6    var message = @"GET $query HTTP/1.1\r\nHost: $host\r\n\r\n";
```

Here we specify the host and port to connect to and construct the HTTP 1.1 GET request:

```
1    GET /v1/current.json?key=<apikey>&q=Paris
2    Host: api.apixu.com
```

Now we need to connect to the server, send the request, receive and parse the answer:

```
1    var resolver = Resolver.get_default();
2    var addresses = resolver.lookup_by_name( host, null );
3    var address = addresses.nth_data( 0 );
4    stderr.printf( @"Resolved $host to $address\n" );
```

As previously mentioned, networking APIs deal with IP addresses rather than human-friendly hostnames, so we first have to resolve the hostname to an IP address. gio provides a Resolver class which can be used for the lookup. Since more than just one IP address can be assigned to every server, we're taking the first IP address.

Note   You may wonder why we don't have to state using Gio or add the prefix Gio: Although gio is technically a separate library from glib, they belong to the same umbrella project and hence are somewhat coupled. This is the reason why its entities in gio-2.0.vapi have been defined within the GLib namespace.

```
1   var client = new SocketClient();
2   var addr = new InetSocketAddress( address, port );
3   var conn = client.connect( addr );
4   stderr.printf( @"Connected to $host\n" );
```

HTTP is a connection-oriented protocol based on TCP. gio provides the class SocketClient for those protocols. The InetSocketAddress is created using the previously resolved address and the specified port. With the connect() call, a TCP connection is opened and wrapped in the return object of type SocketConnection:

```
1   conn.output_stream.write( message.data );
2   stderr.printf( @"Wrote request $message\n" );
```

A SocketConnection is derived from IOStream, which encapsulates a transport stream that can be written to and read from. Here we use its output_stream to send the assembled GET request. Since write() has been designed to work with both text and binary protocols, it takes a uint8[]— therefore we have to use the data property, which returns the actual byte buffer of our string:

```
1   var response = new DataInputStream( conn.input_stream );
2   var status_line = response.read_line( null ).strip();
3   stderr.printf( @"Received status line: '$status_line'\n" );
```

To read bytes from the response, we create a DataInputStream that reads from the connection input. The canonical format of an HTTP response has three parts: First, there is a status line, then a number of header lines, and, last but not least, after an empty line, the response body:

```
1   HTTP/1.1 <Numerical Status Code> <Textual Status Code>
2   <Header>: <Value>
3   ... (more headers)
4
5   <Response Body>
```

We read the first line using read_line(), strip() all whitespace, and assign it to the variable status_line:

```
1  if ( ! ( "200" in status_line ) )
2  {
3  error( "Service did not answer with 200 OK" );
4  }
```

The HTTP status_line we just read indicates whether the actual HTTP request has been processed correctly or not. The status code 200 is an indicator for a positive result.

Afterward, we read and parse the header lines to get the actual content length of the HTTP body:

```
1   var headers = new HashTable<string,string>( str_hash,
    str_equal );
2   var line = "";
3   while ( line != "\r" )
4   {
5       line = response.read_line( null );
6       var headerComponents = line.strip().split( ":", 2 );
7       if ( headerComponents.length == 2 )
8       {
9           var header = headerComponents[0].strip();
10          var value = headerComponents[1].strip();
11          headers[ header ] = value;
12          stderr.printf( @"Got Header: $header = $value\n" );
13      }
14  }
15  var contentLength = headers[ "Content-Length" ].to_int();
```

Although this simple example does not use more than just one header line, let's discuss how we could store all the headers in a data structure:

```
1   var headers = new HashTable<string,string>( str_hash,
    str_equal );
```

Since HTTP header lines are essentially key/value pairs without a meaningful order, a HashTable seems appropriate. HashTable is a generic datatype; hence we have to supply the type of the keys (string), the type of the values (string as well), and matching functions to *hash* and *compare* the values.

For the most basic types, glib already comes with sufficient helper functions for hashing and comparing values, that is, for strings there are str_hash and str_equal. For custom data types, you will have to provide your own functions:

```
1   while ( line != "\r" )
2   {
3       line = response.read_line( null );
```

We loop over all lines until we get an empty line, which denotes the end of the header part in an HTTP response. Note that although the HTTP line terminator is \r\n, we compare the line only against \r here, since read_line() already swallows the \n:

```
1   var headerComponents = line.strip().split( ":", 2 );
2   if ( headerComponents.length == 2 )
3   {
4       var header = headerComponents[0].strip();
5       var value = headerComponents[1].strip();
```

As per the HTTP definition, header lines separate the key and value parts with a colon (:); therefore we split() every string to get a maximum of two components. If we got a well-formatted header line, then we grab the header name and the header value from the component array. We're not interested in leading or trailing whitespace; hence strip() is called on both values:

```
1              headers[ header ] = value;
2              stderr.printf( @"Got Header: $header = $value\n" );
3         }
4    }
5    var contentLength = headers[ "Content-Length" ].to_int();
```

Vala supports the subscript operator for HashTable objects. We use this to look up the HTTP body content length, which—by definition—is contained in the header Content-Length. We could also probe for any other headers just by referring to them via key:

```
1   var jsonResponse = new uint8[ contentLength ];
2   size_t actualLength = 0;
3   response.read_all( jsonResponse, out actualLength );
```

After the HTTP header part, the body part of the HTTP response starts. Since we already know (by peeking into the Content-Length header) how many bytes to expect, we allocate a buffer of sufficient length and read the maximum number of expected bytes with read_all():

```
1   stderr.printf( @"Got $contentLength bytes of JSON
    response: %s\n", jsonResponse );
2   stdout.printf( @"%s", jsonResponse );
```

To allow processing the jsonResponse further, we print it to the standard output. Running this on my machine produces the following result (yes, another usual cold and windy day in Germany):

```
1   $ ./weatherClient | ./jsonParser
2   Current condition is 'Partly cloudy' with 11.0°C,
    feeling like 6.6°C
```

libsoup

In the previous section, we have manually constructed our HTTP request payload. A higher level of abstraction can be achieved using libsoup, which is an HTTP library for GNOME.

As an example for using libsoup, we will now write an HTTP client that gathers our publicly visible IP address using the web service at api. ipify.org.

Example: HTTP Client with libsoup

```
1    var url = "https://api.ipify.org?format=text";
```

The API for ipify allows to specify the output format. Among others, they support plain text and JSON. Since we already demonstrated how to communicate with JSON web services, we don't have to show this again, and will rather request a plain text result:

```
1    var session = new Soup.Session();
```

When using libsoup, the first thing you need to create is a Soup. Session object:

```
1    var message = new Soup.Message( "GET", url );
```

A Soup.Message is an abstraction of an HTTP request. Here we create a GET request using the specified url:

```
1    session.send_message( message );
```

One session object allows us to send any number of messages to a single or multiple hosts. send_message sends the message and blocks further processing until it has received the answer:

```
1    var body = (string) message.response_body.data;
2    print( @"My public IP address is '$body'\n" );
```

The response data is contained in the response_body, which is an object of the type Soup. MessageBody. It provides the response bytes in data and the respective length in length.

Running this program (don't forget to add the necessary --pkg command-line argument) leads to the following output on my machine:

```
1    $ vala --pkg=libsoup-2.4 ipifyClient.vala
2    My public IP address is '130.180.126.235'
```

Note the amount of code lines using libsoup has saved us, sparing us from IP address resolution and manually constructing the HTTP request.

Summary

In this chapter, we have introduced network programming with Vala. We started with using POSIX APIs to communicate with an NTP server, moved over to gio downloading a JSON weather report via HTTP, and finished by using the high-level library libsoup.

CHAPTER 6

UI Programming with GTK+

Nothing travels faster than the speed of light with the possible exception of bad news, which obeys its own special laws.

—Douglas Adams, The Hitchhiker's Guide to the Galaxy

This chapter discusses UI programming with Vala using GTK+ 3.0. After introducing the basic principles of event-driven systems (with UI programming being one of the major applications), we will present an application combining several aspects learned in the previous chapters, for example, network transfers and JSON parsing.

Event-Driven Systems

An *event-driven system* is a system where an event, such as the change of a state, triggers a computational unit, for example, a function. The heart of every event-driven system is an *event loop* that listens for events from all kind of sources (mouse movement, clicks, keyboard input, networking, timers, etc.). The system is designed around the idea that *interested parties* (read: computational units) can subscribe for certain events and will get notified (read: run) when a matching event has been triggered.

© Michael Lauer 2019
M. Lauer, *Introducing Vala Programming*, https://doi.org/10.1007/978-1-4842-5380-9_6

Event-driven systems are the preferred way for handling user interactions. A *user interface library* (also called *UI toolkit*), such as GTK+, implements such an event-driven system with an event loop and facilities for managing graphical entities, such as labels, buttons, lists, text edit fields, and the like.

Every recent proprietary graphical operating system platform (such as Microsoft Windows or Apple macOS) comes with its own *native* UI toolkit. UNIX-like systems originated in a time period where the command line was the only means of user interaction; hence for these, there is no such thing as a native UI toolkit.[1]

Over the years, many competing toolkits have been written for open (and closed) systems; some of these are available for multiple platforms, thus allowing *cross-platform* development—notable ones include

- Qt

- FLTK

- wxWidgets

- JUCE, and, last but not least,

- GTK+.

While all UI toolkits have a native programming language to develop graphical applications (this is, of course, the one used to write the toolkit itself), many also support a number of bindings for other languages.

---

[1]You could consider xlib being the native UI toolkit for systems running an X-Window display server; however xlib is such a low-level library that the categorization "toolkit" would be very euphemistic.

GTK+

GTK+ was initially developed in the mid-1990s, as part of the *GNU Image Manipulation Program (GIMP)*. It has been written and C and was eventually ported to other platforms. It is mainly used in the GNOME project.

GTK+ is a feature-rich toolkit containing a comprehensive collection of widgets, allowing to write all kinds of simple and complex desktop applications. In this chapter, we will present a small (but not trivial) example application that uses many techniques presented in earlier chapters.

Example: Streaming Radio Client

Overview

This application will be called "NetRadio"—a streaming radio client for the Internet. NetRadio will allow the user to browse through a set of radio stations and genres, provided by a JSON web service.[2] When a station is picked, a connection to the station will be opened, and audio will be heard.

User Interface

It is always advisable to think about *what* to build, before considering *how* to build it—especially when it comes to developing a UI application. Before implementing a user interface, it is useful to scribble some (naturally static) *mockups* that show the application parts in different states and then derive a set of *user stories*—or vice versa.

---

[2]Previous editions of this book used the Dirble Internet radio station directory, which unfortunately has been offline for a while now.

Let's start with a handful of user stories for NetRadio:

1. The user would like to browse through available radio station genres.

2. The user would like to browse through stations belonging to a selected genre.

3. The user would like to "tune in" to one station.

4. The user would like to pause and resume the currently playing station.

Based on these stories, we decide that the user interface should have three areas, for *navigation, content,* and *action*:

Navigation: This should explain what we are currently seeing in the content area and provide a way to navigate "back" one level.

Content: This should contain the list of things to choose of, either genres or stations.

Action: This should allow actions with a selected station.

Here is a scribble for NetRadio (Figure 6-1).

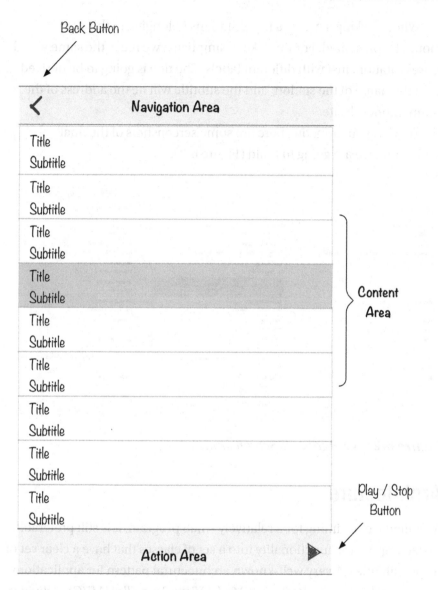

Figure 6-1. *NetRadio UI Scribble*

Since the user should be able to browse through a list of genres, we need to think about how we want to represent one genre. Most genres have a title and a description; hence we go for two lines of text.

When clicking a genre, a list of stations belonging to this genre should be presented. For the sake of simplicity, we reuse the same visual representation, just with different labels. The title is going to be derived from the name of the station, and the subtitle will be the address of the companion web site.

To whet your appetite, here are some screenshots of the final application we are going to build (Figure 6-2).

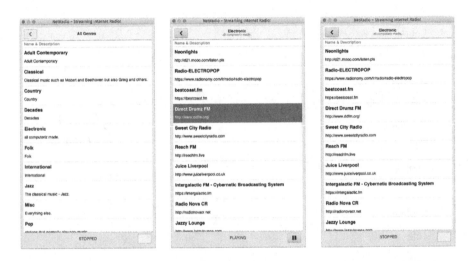

Figure 6-2. *NetRadio UI Screenshots*

Architecture

Although we're aiming for a relatively small program, it is still preferable to decompose the functionality into a set of classes that have a clear set of responsibilities. A very well-known architectural pattern for applications with a graphical user interface is *Model View Controller (MVC)*. It divides the classes into three set of categories, *model classes*, *view classes*, and *controller classes*:

- **Model classes**: Contain data, that is, represent our genres and our stations.

- **View classes**: Handle the visual representation of the data, that is, labels and buttons.

- **Controller classes**: Handle the navigation (i.e., user events) between parts of the application and the flow of data.

Although MVC has not generally guided the development of GTK+, we would still like to base our application structure on it.

Here is an overview of all the NetRadio classes that we're about to present (Figure 6-3).

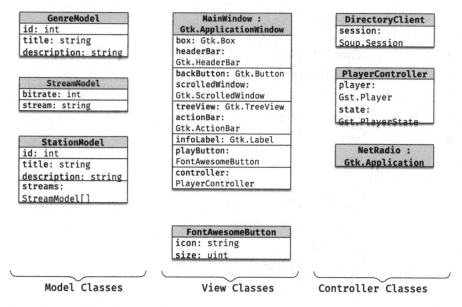

Figure 6-3. NetRadio Classes

Model Classes Since most of the data is downloaded from the radio station directory web service, we can derive the model classes by looking at the JSON responses. To do this, I recommend using a command-line HTTP transfer application, such as wget, curl, or http.

Let's take a look at the JSON format for genres:

```
 1   $ http https://wellenreiter.vanille.de/netradio/genres
 2
 3   [
 4       {
 5           "count": 150,
 6           "haschildren": true,
 7           "id": 1,
 8           "name": "Alternative",
 9           "parentid": 0
10       },
11       {
12           "count": 5583,
13           "haschildren": true,
14           "id": 24,
15           "name": "Blues",
16           "parentid": 0
17       },
18       {
19           "count": 1386,
20           "haschildren": true,
21           "id": 32,
22           "name": "Classical",
23           "parentid": 0
24       },
25       {
26           "count": 2145,
27           "haschildren": true,
28           "id": 44,
29           "name": "Country",
30           "parentid": 0
31       },
```

```
32        {
33            "count": 102,
34            "haschildren": true,
35            "id": 212,
36            "name": "Decades",
37            "parentid": 0
38        },
39
40        . . . . . . . .
41    ]
```

Here is an example for gathering the stations for the genre "Alternative," which has the genre id 1:

```
1   $ http https://wellenreiter.vanille.de/netradio/genres/1
2
3   [
4       {
5           "br": 128,
6           "ct": "Denis Ramniceanu - Petrece Romaneste -
                  FMRadioManele.Ro",
7           "genre": "International",
8           "genre2": "Top 40",
9           "genre3": "Oldies",
10          "genre4": "Indie Rock",
11          "id": 1454276,
12          "lc": 1650,
13          "logo": "http://i.radionomy.com/document/
                    radios/9/934a/934a38ef-f874-4be2-bf1d-
                    456962f053f4.png",
14          "ml": 4700,
15          "mt": "audio/mpeg",
```

```
16              "name": "Radio Manele Romania www.FMRadioManele.Ro"
17          },
18          {
19              "br": 192,
20              "ct": "PIONEER REC - REC006 [7F5]",
21              "genre": "Hardcore",
22              "id": 1638033,
23              "lc": 1218,
24              "ml": 6000,
25              "mt": "audio/mpeg",
26              "name": "Pure Radio Holland - Hardcore Channel
                        (192 kbps)"
27          },
28          {
29              "br": 64,
30              "ct": "Club 8 - You Could Be Anybody",
31              "genre": "Misc",
32              "genre2": "Easy Listening",
33              "genre3": "Electronic",
34              "genre4": "Pop",
35              "genre5": "Indie Pop",
36              "id": 1264969,
37              "lc": 440,
38              "logo": "http://i.radionomy.com/document/radios/b/
                        b2c5/b2c582af-0cc8-418c-bc25-cea5e86c780a.
                        png",
39              "ml": 1200,
40              "mt": "audio/aacp",
41              "name": "Soundstorm-radio.com Relax Radio -
                        Electronic Pop Indie World"
42          },
```

```
43    {
44        "br": 128,
45        "genre": "Rock",
46        "genre2": "Electronic",
47        "genre3": "Drum and Bass",
48        "genre4": "Indie Rock",
49        "genre5": "Experimental",
50        "id": 1693740,
51        "lc": 361,
52        "logo": "http://i.radionomy.com/document/radios/f/
                 f8fd/f8fd8583-65f5-41a0-938b-131361b0db1e.
                 png",
53        "ml": 500,
54        "mt": "audio/mpeg",
55        "name": "Radio Kampus 97,1 FM"
56    },
57    . . . . . . .
58  ]
```

To gather the actual streaming URL from a station, we need the
following call:

```
1   $ http https://wellenreiter.vanille.de/netradio/
    stations/1693740
2
3   {
4       "url": "http://193.0.98.66:8005"
5   }
```

Analyzing these responses, it becomes obvious that we can model the most important properties by defining the two model classes GenreModel and StationModel:

- GenreModel encapsulates a genre, such as "Country."

- StationModel represents a station, such as "Radio Kampus 97,1 FM."

All of these look pretty similar; hence we will only show the GenreModel here:

```
1   public class GenreModel : Object
2   {
3       public int id { get; private set; }
4       public string title { get; private set; }
5       public string description { get; private set; }
6   }
```

GenreModel has three important fields, which we have modeled as read-only automatic properties (note the **private** set):[3]

1. An integer identification id (necessary for querying the stations belonging to a certain genre)

2. A string title text

3. A string description text

Since these model classes primarily exist to hold data (fed by JSON), in general we only need one constructor, which, given a Json.Object, initializes the instance:

```
1   public GenreModel.fromJsonObject( Json.Object json )
2   {
```

---

[3]Here, we might have also used GObject-style construct properties which are immutable and guaranteed to be set during object initialization.

```
3        this.id = (int) json.get_int_member( "id" );
4        this.title = json.get_string_member( "name" );
5        var count = json.get_int_member( "count" );
6        this.description = @"$count stations in genre";
7    }
```

In the constructor fromJsonObject(), we take the values out of the Json.Object and assign them to the variables backing our class properties.

View Classes For this example, we only need two view classes, FontAwesomeButton and MainWindow:

- FontAwesomeButton is a special button derived from the standard GTK+ Button class. It renders an icon out of the great FontAwesome icon collection.

- MainWindow contains the widgets that make up our layout. It sets up the content, handles user input, and coordinates the data flow from/to the controller classes.

Let's briefly present FontAwesomeButton as a simple example for a custom widget:

```
1    class FontAwesomeButton : Gtk.Button
2    {
3        private string _icon;
4        private uint _size;
5
6        public FontAwesomeButton( uint size, string icon )
7        {
8            Object( label: "dummy" );
9            _size = size;
10           this.icon = icon;
11       }
12   }
```

The default constructor takes a size parameter and an icon string. FontAwesome comes with a TrueType font where the individual glyphs are mapped to characters. We need to make sure that our system has installed the FontAwesome.ttf, thus sparing us from integrating all the individual icon files we may want to show. We chain to the superclass constructor by using the generic GLib.Object class that allows us to initialize any number of properties with one call. From the constructor, we call the icon property setter that does the actual work:

```
1   public string icon
2   {
3       get
4       {
5           return _icon;
6       }
7       set
8       {
9           var label = (Gtk.Label) get_child();
10          var markup = @"<span font_desc=\"FontAwesome $_
            size\">$value</span>";
11          label.set_markup( markup );
12      }
13  }
```

The getter just returns the private variable backing the property. The setter takes a reference to the one and only child of the Gtk.Button, which is a Gtk.Label—a label that supports both plain text and (a limited form of) HTML/CSS markup.

The easiest way to render the required glyph is to construct an HTML string, such as the following:

```
1   <span font_desc="FontAwesome 16">&#61523;</span>
```

Setting this with set_markup() will result in a chevron (<) pointing to the left.

Let's discuss the largest class in this example now. For the main window widget setup and the input/output logic, we derive our custom view class MainWindow from Gtk.ApplicationWindow, which is the base class for top-level windows belonging to a companion Gtk.Application object:

```
1    class MainWindow : Gtk.ApplicationWindow
2    {
3        private Gtk.Box _box;                        // WIDGETS
4        private Gtk.HeaderBar _headerBar;
5        private Gtk.Button _backButton;
6        private Gtk.ScrolledWindow _scrolledWindow;
7        private Gtk.TreeView _treeView;
8        private Gtk.ActionBar _actionBar;
9        private Gtk.Label _infoLabel;
10       private FontAwesomeButton _playButton;
11
12       private PlayerController _controller;    // CONTROLLER
13
14       private GenreModel[]? _genres;           // MODEL
15       private GenreModel? _genre;
16       private StationModel[]? _stations;
17       private StationModel _station;
18
19       private bool initialSelectionHack;       // MISC
20   }
```

We create the necessary member variables to hold references to widgets, controller classes, and model classes.

The constructor is quite large, since it does all the setup work:

```
1    public MainWindow( Gtk.Application app, string title )
2    {
3        Object( application: app, title: title );
4
5        _box = new Gtk.Box( Gtk.Orientation.VERTICAL, 0 );
6        _box.homogeneous = false;
7        add( _box );
8
9        _headerBar = new Gtk.HeaderBar();
10       _box.pack_start( _headerBar, false, false );
11
12       _backButton = new FontAwesomeButton( 18, "&#61523;" );
13       _backButton.clicked.connect( onBackButtonClicked );
14       _headerBar.pack_start( _backButton );
15
16       _scrolledWindow = new Gtk.ScrolledWindow( null, null );
17       _box.pack_start( _scrolledWindow, true, true );
18
19       _treeView = new Gtk.TreeView();
20       _treeView.set_grid_lines( Gtk.TreeViewGridLines.
         HORIZONTAL );
21       _treeView.activate_on_single_click = true;
22       _treeView.get_selection().changed.connect(onTreeView
         SelectionChanged );
23
24       var cell = new Gtk.CellRendererText();
25       cell.set_padding( 4, 10 );
```

```
26        _treeView.insert_column_with_attributes(
27            -1, "Name & Description", cell, "markup", 0 );
28        _scrolledWindow.add( _treeView );
29
30        _actionBar = new Gtk.ActionBar();
31        _box.pack_start( _actionBar, false, false );
32
33        _infoLabel = new Gtk.Label( "" );
34        _actionBar.set_center_widget( _infoLabel );
35        _playButton = new FontAwesomeButton( 18, "&#61515;" );
36        _playButton.clicked.connect( onPlayButtonClicked );
37        _actionBar.pack_end( _playButton );
38
39        _controller = new PlayerController();
40        _controller.didUpdateGenres.connect(
              onControllerDidUpdateGenres );
41        _controller.didUpdateStations.connect(
              onControllerDidUpdateStations );
42        _controller.didUpdatePlayerState.connect(
              onControllerDidUpdatePlayerState );
43
44        _controller.loadPrimaryCategories();
45    }
```

Don't worry though, we will now discuss this, piece by piece:

```
1    public MainWindow( Gtk.Application app, string title )
2    {
3        Object( application: app, title: title );
```

The constructor takes two parameters: a reference to the application class and a window title. The window title is not shown by GTK+ but rather provided to the platform's window manager (not all platforms are honoring this). Again, we use the generic GLib.Object constructor to initialize the necessary properties of the superclass:

```
1   _box = new Gtk.Box( Gtk.Orientation.VERTICAL, 0 );
2   _box.homogeneous = false;
3   add( _box );
```

As mentioned before, GTK+ handles its layout as a hierarchy of widgets contained in top-level windows. A major concept for that layout is the *container widget* (represented as the class Gtk.Container), which serves as a container for other widgets. A container for simple layouts is Gtk.Box, which lays out its children either horizontally or vertically. We aim for a vertical layout here; hence we supply Gtk.Orientation.VERTICAL. The second parameter is an additional margin (graphical padding in number of pixels) between the children.

Gtk.Box uses several hints to determine the sizing of its children. Since we chose a vertical layout, all children will have the full width of the container widget. We do not want to have all children the same height (the content area should take more space than the other areas); hence we set homogenous to **false**.

Gtk.ApplicationWindow derives from Gtk.Bin, which is a special Gtk. Container that takes only one child. The _box we have just created will be the child of our MainWindow. The method add() is coming from Gtk. Container and adds a child to a container:

```
1   _headerBar = new Gtk.HeaderBar();
2   _box.pack_start( _headerBar, false, false );
3
4   _backButton = new FontAwesomeButton( 18, "&#61523;" );
5   _backButton.clicked.connect( onBackButtonClicked );
6   _headerBar.pack_start( _backButton );
```

In the navigation area, we would like to show a title and a subtitle. This can easily be done using Gtk. HeaderBar, which supports a number of widgets in front of (pack_start()) and/or after (pack_end ()) the centered title and subtitle. We create an instance of the header and store it in _headerBar. Then we add it to the _box container: pack_start() from Gtk.Box takes three parameters:

1. The child widget to add

2. Whether to expand if extra space is available

3. Whether to dedicate the extra space to the widget's content or to use the extra space for padding

In order to navigate "backward" in our application (i.e., move from the list of stations back to the list of genres), we add a dedicated button to the Gtk.HeaderBar. This button is an instance of the aforementioned FontAwesomeButton—our custom widget derived from Gtk.Button. All GTK+ buttons have a clicked signal that is emitted when the user interacts with the button (either by clicking a mouse, tapping on a touch pad, or—when the widget has the keyboard input focus—using the keyboard). We connect this signal to the helper function onBackButtonClicked(), which we will discuss later:

```
1   _scrolledWindow = new Gtk.ScrolledWindow( null, null );
2   _box.pack_start( _scrolledWindow, true, true );
3   _treeView = new Gtk.TreeView();
4   _scrolledWindow.add( _treeView );
```

The central part of the layout is the list of genres, respectively, stations. A suitable widget for displaying lists (and trees) is Gtk.TreeView. This widget adjusts its size based on its content, which might be undesirable, since the sizing of top-level windows is usually up to the user. For cases like this, GTK+ has a Gtk.ScrolledWindow, which shows only a part of its child. The user can then select the visible part by scrolling up and down and/or left and right. As the scrolled window should occupy all the available extra space of its parent Gtk.Box, this time we provide **true** as the parameters to pack_start():

```
1   _treeView.set_grid_lines( Gtk.TreeViewGridLines.HORIZONTAL );
2   _treeView.activate_on_single_click = true;
3   _treeView.get_selection().changed.connect(
    onTreeViewSelectionChanged );
4   var cell = new Gtk.CellRendererText();
5   cell.set_padding( 4, 10 );
6   _treeView.insert_column_with_attributes(
7       -1,
8       "Name & Description",
9       cell,
10      "markup",
11      0 );
```

Here we configure the Gtk.TreeView: First, we enable horizontal grid lines, and then we activate the single click mode. To get notified of a changed selection, we connect our method onTreeViewSelectionChanged() to the changed signal of Gtk. TreeSelection. Whenever the user adjusts the selection now, our method is run.

As previously mentioned, the architectural pattern MVC has not generally guided the GTK+ development—however, Gtk.TreeView is a notable exception as it contains different kinds of *storage models* (model classes) and *cell renderers* (view classes) that can be used for displaying structured data. The content is provided in terms of rows and columns.

Every column can have a dedicated cell renderer. This lets you easily show, for example, an image in the first column, a text in the second column, a check box in the third column, and so on.

In our case, we only need one column with text, for both genres and stations. Consequently, we create an instance of a Gtk.CellRendererText, insert padding to make the text breathe a bit, and create a column by calling insert_column_with_attributes():

```
1    _actionBar = new Gtk.ActionBar();
2    _box.pack_start( _actionBar, false, false );
3
4    _infoLabel = new Gtk.Label( "" );
5    _actionBar.set_center_widget( _infoLabel );
6    _playButton = new FontAwesomeButton( 18, "&#61515;" );
7    _playButton.clicked.connect( onPlayButtonClicked );
8    _actionBar.pack_end( _playButton );
```

Finally, we configure the lower part of our layout. This is supposed to carry a status text and a button to play/pause the currently playing station. The Gtk.ActionBar is a layout widget that carries a number of children (similar to a Gtk.Box with horizontal orientation) but also designates an optional *center* widget, which is positioned in the center and gets all the remaining extra space.

We instantiate this object and add it to our main Gtk.Box with pack_start(). For the status text, we create a simple Gtk.Label and set it as the action bar's center widget. Furthermore, we construct another FontAwesomeButton, connect() its clicked signal to another callback, and add it to the right side of the action bar using pack_end():

```
1        _controller = new PlayerController();
2        _controller.didUpdateGenres.connect( onController
         DidUpdateGenres );
```

```
3        _controller.didUpdateStations.connect( onControllerDid
         UpdateStations );
4        _controller.didUpdatePlayerState.connect( onController
         DidUpdatePlayerState );
5
6        _controller.loadPrimaryCategories();
7    }
```

After all this UI setup, we need a `PlayerController` (see the following discussion), which is going to manage the actual playing of the Internet radio station. Whenever the `PlayerController` has loaded a new set of genres or stations, it emits the signal `didUpdateGenres,` respectively, `didUpdateStations`. We `connect()` to these signals.

You may wonder "Wouldn't it be easier to simply return the genres in the call `loadPrimaryCategories` `()`?" This is due to our preferred asynchronous communication style: Loading the categories will invoke a network call which may take some time to respond. We do not want to block the constructor for that time frame. GTK+ does all its work in the event loop, which only runs *after* the constructor returns. If we were to block during the constructor, the application window would neither be visible nor responsive to user events—until the network call has finished.

We still need to discuss the signal handlers and a bunch of helpers methods in the `MainWindow` class. We will roughly follow the user's logical flow through the application. The last action in the constructor was calling the controller's `loadPrimaryCategories()`. We will later discuss how this works internally, but for now let's assume that this method did its work and afterward emits the signal `didUpdateGenres`, which leads to `onControllerDidUpdateGenres` being called:

```
1    private void onControllerDidUpdateGenres( GenreModel[]
     genres )
2    {
```

```
3         _genres = genres;
4         _stations = null;
5         updateUI();
6     }
```

We save the received genres in our private member variable, mark the stations as **null,** and call the helper method updateUI:

```
1   private void updateUI()
2   {
3       updateHeader();
4       updateList();
5       updateActionBar();
6   }
```

This in turn calls three helper methods that update the navigation area, the content area, and the action area, respectively:

```
1   private void updateHeader()
2   {
3       if ( _genre != null )
4       {
5           _headerBar.title = _genre.title;
6           _headerBar.subtitle = _genre.description;
7           _backButton.sensitive = true;
8       }
9       else
10      {
11          _headerBar.title = "All Genres";
12          _headerBar.subtitle = null;
13          _backButton.sensitive = false;
14      }
15  }
```

Although most Internet radio dictionaries actually support a tree of genres (i.e., primary genres, secondary genres, and for some genres even more layer), for the sake of simplicity, we restrict ourselves to deal only with primary genres and stations in this application.

Once a genre is selected, the member variable _genre is set to a value other than **null**. We can then be sure that the content area contains the list of stations; hence we set the Gtk.HeaderBar title to the currently selected genre's title.

If _genre is **null** though, no genre has been selected yet. This means that the content area shows the list of primary genres; thus we set the title to a fixed string. The _backButton should only be sensitive (which is the GTK+ term for "enabled," hence clickable) when it is possible to go back, that is, when a list of stations is shown.

Updating the content area is more complex:

```
1    private void updateList()
2    {
3        var listmodel = new Gtk.ListStore( 1, typeof(string) );
4        _treeView.set_model( listmodel );
```

As mentioned before, Gtk.TreeView can use a storage model. In this case, we create a Gtk. ListStore that features a single text column (hence the string type). This model is then set on the widget using set_model():

```
1    Gtk.TreeIter iter;
2    if ( _stations == null )
3    {
4        for( int i = 0; i < _genres.length; ++i )
5        {
6            listmodel.append( out iter );
7            var title = markupSanitize( _genres[i].title );
8            var subtitle = markupSanitize( _genres[i].
             description );
```

```
 9              if ( subtitle.length == 0 )
10              {
11                  subtitle = title;
12              }
13              var str = "<big><b>%s</b></big>\n\n%s".printf
                ( title, subtitle );
14              listmodel.set( iter, 0, str );
15          }
16      }
```

If there are no _stations, we will need to show the list of genres: The
for loop iterates over all genres and creates and appends the necessary
list model data based on the genre's title and its description. While
all genres have a title, some are lacking a description. If this is the case,
duplicating the title leads to a prettier list.

Similar to a Gtk.Label, the Gtk.CellRendererText features not only
plain text but also HTML markup. We construct a markup string similar to
the following:

```
1    <big><b>title</b></big>\n\n%s
```

This markup string displays the text in two lines, with the title being
bigger and bolder than the subtitle.

Since we don't know the actual contents of title and description,
they might contain strings that could be misinterpreted when taken
verbatim. On this behalf, we wrote the helper method markupSanitize()
which scans through a string and returns an HTML-compatible version.[4]

---

[4]In general it is considered good practice to clean up (filter) strings downloaded
from the network before they get fed to code that might (mis)-interpret certain
characters as control sequences.

The constructed string is then set() as the row data for the list model:

```
1       else
2       {
3           for( int i = 0; i < _stations.length; ++i )
4           {
5               listmodel.append( out iter );
6               var title = markupSanitize( _stations[i].name );
7               var subtitle = markupSanitize( _stations[i].
                website );
8               var str = "<big><b>%s</b></big>\n\n%s".
                printf( title, subtitle );
9               listmodel.set( iter, 0, str );
10          }
11      }
12  }
```

The **else** case is run when we need to show the list of stations rather than the list of genres. This is pretty similar to the genre case: We loop over the _stations and use the station's name and website to construct the markup string.

Next, we will update the action area, in particular the text label and the play/pause button:

```
1   private void updateActionBar()
2   {
3       string stateString = "";
4
5       switch ( _controller.state )
6       {
7           case Gst.PlayerState.STOPPED:
8               stateString = "STOPPED";
9               _playButton.icon = "";
```

```
10                     _playButton.set_sensitive( false );
11               break;
12
13           case Gst.PlayerState.BUFFERING:
14               stateString = "BUFFERING...";
15               _playButton.icon = "&#61712;";
16               _playButton.set_sensitive( false );
17               break;
18
19           case Gst.PlayerState.PAUSED:
20               stateString = "PAUSED";
21               _playButton.icon = "&#61515;";
22               _playButton.set_sensitive( true );
23               break;
24
25           case Gst.PlayerState.PLAYING:
26               stateString = "PLAYING";
27               _playButton.icon = "&#61516;";
28               _playButton.set_sensitive( true );
29               break;
30       }
31
32       var str = @"$stateString";
33       _infoLabel.set_markup( str );
34   }
```

The playing state can be gathered by inspecting the state property of
the instance of our PlayerController. It informs us about what to show
in the label, the icon of the play/pause button, and whether that button
should be enabled or not.

This concludes the discussion of the updateUI() helper methods. Next, we will look the event handlers, that is, our methods that have been connected to signals:

```
1    private void onTreeViewSelectionChanged()
2    {
3        Gtk.TreeModel model;
4        var paths = _treeView.get_selection().get_selected_
         rows( out model );
5        if ( paths.length() == 0 )
6        {
7            return;
8        }
9        Gtk.TreePath path = paths.first().data;
10       int[] indices = path.get_indices();
11       var rowIndex = indices[0];
12
13       if ( _genre == null )
14       {
15           _genre = _genres[rowIndex];
16           _controller.loadStationsForGenre( _genre );
17       }
18       else // stations are in
19       {
20           _station = _stations[rowIndex];
21           _controller.playStation( _station );
22       }
23   }
```

The method onTreeViewSelectionChanged() is called when the user selects a row in the list widget Gtk.TreeView. As this widget supports multiple selection, we first have to gather a list of selected rows. If there are none, we **return** early.

The first Gtk.TreePath contains the index for the first (and in our case, only) selected row. To derive the actually selected genre or station from this rowIndex, we have to distinguish between showing a list of genres vs. showing a list of stations again: If we have no selected _genre, we are displaying the list of genres. We set _genre to the selected genre and call the method loadStationsForGenre () on the controller to load the stations belonging to that genre. In the other case, we instruct the controller to play the selected station by calling playStation():

```
1    private void onBackButtonClicked()
2    {
3        _genre = null;
4        _stations = null;
5        updateUI();
6    }
```

If the back button is clicked, the event handler onBackButtonClicked() gets called. This can only happen when the list of stations is displayed in the content area, that is, the primary genres have already been loaded. To have the list of genres reappear, we only need to clear the selected _genre, set the _stations to null, and call updateUI() again:

```
1    private void onPlayButtonClicked()
2    {
3        _controller.togglePlayPause();
4    }
```

The event handler onPlayButtonClicked() gets called when the play/pause button is clicked. In that case, we call the controller's togglePlayPause() (which will lead to a state change, eventually resulting in an adjusted icon for the button):

```
1    private void onPlayerStateChanged()
2    {
3        updateActionBar();
4    }
```

Last but not least, the method onPlayerStateChanged() will be called when the player controller's state changes. This does not have any effect on the navigation area or content area, so that we only have to update the action area by calling updateActionBar().

Controller Classes: The controller classes for this project are PlayerController and DirectoryClient:

- PlayerController contains the "business logic" for the MainWindow and provides APIs for loading genres, loading stations, and playing a station.

- DirectoryClient handles the actual communication with the Internet radio station directory web service and transforms the JSON answers into our model classes.

Let's start with the PlayerController:

```
1    class PlayerController : Object
2    {
3        private Gst.Player _player;
4        private Gst.PlayerState _state;
5        private DirectoryClient _directoryClient;
```

We derive PlayerController from GLib.Object, since we want to use signals and properties. For playing an audio stream, the class holds the two member variables _player and _state:

- Gst.Player is a class from the multimedia framework gstreamer.[5] It wraps all the low-level details of handling Internet radio streams and the audio hardware.

- Gst.PlayerState is an enumeration representing the different states of the audio streaming engine, most notable BUFFERING, PLAYING, and PAUSED.

The member variable _directoryClient holds a reference to the DirectoryClient that handles the communication with the Internet radio station directory web service:

```
1   public signal void didUpdateGenres( GenreModel[] genres );
2   public signal void didUpdateStations( StationModel[]
    stations );
3   public signal void didUpdatePlayerState();
```

We declare three signals:

1. didUpdateGenres, emitted when the (possibly lengthy) genre data transfer has finished

2. didUpdateStations, emitted when the station data transfer has finished

3. didUpdatePlayerState, emitted when the playback state has changed

---

[5]GStreamer is a very flexible set of libraries for constructing graphs of media-handling components. It supports a wide range of applications, from simple audio playback and audio/video streaming to complex audio (mixing) and video (nonlinear editing) processing. For more information, please refer to gstreamer. freedesktop.org.

```
1   public Gst.PlayerState state {
2       get {
3           return _state;
4               }
5       }
```

For some reason, Gst.Player does not contain a property that holds its state. We therefore have to save the state whenever we receive a state change notification from GstPlayer. To please our API consumers, we offer such a property for them. Since state is strictly read-only, we only have to provide a getter.

This concludes our discussion of member variables, signals, and properties. Let's move on to the constructor:

```
1   public PlayerController()
2   {
3       _player = new Gst.Player( null, null );
4       _player.volume = 0.5;
5       _player.state_changed.connect( onPlayerStateChanged );
6
7       _directoryClient = new DirectoryClient();
8   }
```

In the constructor, we create a new Gst.Player instance and lower the volume a bit. We are interested in listening to one signal, namely, state_ changed, which is emitted whenever the (internal) stream playback state changes. We also construct an instance of our DirectoryClient.

In order to forward information about stream playback state changes, the signal handler onPlayerStateChanged() is created in the following way:

```
1   public void onPlayerStateChanged( Gst.PlayerState state )
2   {
3       _state = state;
4       didUpdatePlayerState();
5   }
```

We save the state in our member variable and emit our signal
didUpdatePlayerState(), so that interested parties will get notified.

Let's now discuss the public API of PlayerController. We provide the
following four methods:

1. loadPrimaryCategories(), for loading the primary
   genres

2. loadStationsForGenre(), for loading the stations
   belonging to one genre

3. playStation(), for streaming audio from one station

4. togglePlayPause(), for pausing and resuming the
   audio stream playback

In order to properly implement the first two methods, we need to
introduce a new Vala feature here:

Asynchronous Methods: An asynchronous method is a method that
can halt its execution at "some" point, give control back to the event loop,
and later resume at the point it had paused. This is especially helpful
when writing code that deals with network operations—these usually
have to wait for a response and would otherwise block the main loop from
processing more events in the meantime.

In Vala, asynchronous methods are declared using the async keyword:

```
1   public int async thisIsAnAsynchronousMethod( int someParam )
2   {
3       return someParam;
4   }
```

Within an asynchronous method, the yield keyword is used to specify a halt point and/or call another asynchronous method. In our case we make use of the latter, since the DirectoryClient will also feature asynchronous methods:

```
1    public async void loadPrimaryCategories()
2    {
3        var genres = yield _directoryClient.loadGenres();
4        if ( genres != null )
5        {
6            print( @"Received $(genres.length) genres\n" );
7            didUpdateGenres( genres );
8        }
9        else
10       {
11           warning( @"Could not get genres" );
12       }
13   }
```

loadPrimaryCategories() delegates most of the work to the DirbleClient and calls its corresponding API. Since this is another asynchronous method, we use yield here. If the return value is a non-**null** array of GenreModel objects, we emit the signal didUpdateGenres to notify the subscribers:

```
1    public async void loadStationsForGenre( GenreModel genre )
2    {
3        var stations = yield _directoryClient.loadStations
         ( genre );
4        if ( stations != null )
5        {
6            print( @"Received $(stations.length) stations\n" );
```

```
7            didUpdateStations( stations );
8        }
9    else
10    {
11            warning( @"Could not get stations" );
12    }
13  }
```

Similar to the preceding code, loadStationsForGenre() delegates the work to the DirectoryClient and calls the corresponding (asynchronous) API. If the result is a non-**null** array of StationModel objects, we emit our signal didUpdateStations to notify event listeners:

```
1    public async void playStation( StationModel station )
2    {
3        _player.stop();
4        var url = yield _directoryClient.loadUrlForStation
           ( station );
5        _player.uri = url;
6        print( @"Player URI now $url\n" );
7        _player.play();
8    }
```

playStation() first stops the currently playing station, uses the DirectoryClient to load the a streaming url from the StationModel, sets this as the uri property on the Gst.Player, and finally calls play() to start streaming:

```
1    public void togglePlayPause()
2    {
3        switch ( _state )
4        {
5            case Gst.PlayerState.STOPPED:
```

```
 6                break;
 7
 8          case Gst.PlayerState.BUFFERING:
 9                break;
10
11          case Gst.PlayerState.PAUSED:
12                _player.play();
13                break;
14
15          case Gst.PlayerState.PLAYING:
16                _player.pause();
17                break;
18
19          default:
20                break;
21      }
22  }
```

The method togglePlayPause() is a convenient way to pause and resume the playback of an audio stream. Based on the current _state, it calls the Gst.Player's play() or pause().

The last class to discuss is the controller class DirectoryClient, which takes care of the network communication:

```
1   const string PrefixURL = "https://wellenreiter.vanille.de/
    netradio";
2   const string GetPrimaryCategoriesURL = PrefixURL + "/
    genres";
3   const string GetStationsForGenreURL = PrefixURL + "/
    genres/%u";
4   const string GetStationURL = PrefixURL + "/stations/%u";
```

First, we define the necessary web service URLs. In the case of this service, the prefix is always `https://wellenreiter.vanille.de/netradio`. The path to get the primary genres is `/genres`, while the path to get the stations for a certain genre is `/genres/<genre-id>`:

```
1    delegate void StringCompletionHandler( uint statusCode,
     Json.Node rootNode );
```

This declares a callback method, which we use for an internal helper method returning an HTTP status code and a `Json.Node`:

```
1    public class DirectoryClient : Object
2    {
3        private Soup.Session _session;
4
5        public DirectoryClient()
6        {
7            _session = new Soup.Session();
8        }
9    }
```

For the network transfer, we will again use `libsoup` (see Chapter 5). We declare a `Soup.Session` as a member variable, which gets instantiated in the constructor.

The public API for `DirectoryClient` consists of the following three asynchronous methods:

1. `loadGenres()` loads the list of genres and transforms the JSON answer into an array of `GenreModel` classes.

2. `loadStations()` loads the list of stations and transforms the JSON answer into an array of `StationModel` classes.

3. `loadUrlForStation()` loads the URL for a concrete station.

```
1    public async GenreModel[]? loadGenres()
2    {
3        GenreModel[] result = null;
4
5        var url = GetPrimaryCategoriesURL;
6        loadJsonForURL( url, ( statusCode, rootNode ) => {
7
8            if ( statusCode == 200 )
9            {
10                var genres = new GenreModel[] {};
11                var array = rootNode.get_array();
12                for ( uint i = 0; i < array.get_length(); ++i )
13                {
14                    var object = array.get_object_element( i );
15                    var genre = new GenreModel.fromJsonObject
                        ( object );
16                    genres += genre;
17                }
18                result = genres;
19            }
20        } );
21
22        return result;
23    }
```

The actual loading is done in the loadJsonForURL helper method which we'll discuss in a minute. This method calls a delegate (here specified in place as a lambda method) receiving two parameters: a status code and a Json.Node for the root node. If the status code equals 200 (OK), we build the array of GenreModel objects by iterating through the Json.Array—calling the constructor GenreModel.fromJsonObject() for every member of the array.

We return the constructed array or **null**, if the transfer did not complete successfully (as indicated by an HTTP status code other than 200):

```
1    public async StationModel[]? loadStations( GenreModel genre )
2    {
3        StationModel[] result = null;
4
5        var url = GetStationsForGenreURL.printf( genre.id );
6        loadJsonForURL( url, ( statusCode, rootNode ) => {
7
8            if ( statusCode == 200 )
9            {
10                var stations = new StationModel[] {};
11                var array = rootNode.get_array();
12                for ( uint i = 0; i < array.get_length(); ++i )
13                {
14                    var object = array.get_object_element( i );
15                    var station = new StationModel.fromJson
                        Object( object );
16                    stations += station;
17                }
18                result = stations;
19            }
20
21        } );
22
23        return result;
24    }
```

The method to load stations is pretty similar in style, with the difference being that we construct an array of StationModel instances instead of GenreModel instances.

```
1    public async string? loadUrlForStation( StationModel
     station )
2    {
3        string result = null;
4        var url = GetStationURL.printf( station.id );
5        loadJsonForURL( url, ( statusCode, rootNode ) => {
6
7            if ( statusCode == 200 )
8            {
9                var object = rootNode.get_object();
10               result = object.get_string_member( "url" );
11           }
12
13       } );
14
15       return result;
16   }
```

Loading the URL for a given station is pretty simple as we only have to pick out the value of the url field from the JSON answer. You might ask why the service doesn't simply return the URL instead of a complete object, but this is due to the JSON specification where the permitted top-level structure needs to be OBJECT or ARRAY.

Let's discuss the helper method loadJsonForURL() now:

```
1    public void loadJsonForURL( string url,
     StringCompletionHandler block )
2    {
3        var message = new Soup.Message( "GET", url );
4        assert( message != null );
5        _session.send_message( message );
6        print( "GET %s => %u\n%s\n",
```

```
7            url,
8            message.status_code,
9            (string) message.response_body.data );
10       var rootnode = Json.from_string( (string) message.
         response_body. data );
11       block( message.status_code, rootnode    );
12   }
```

A Soup.Message is constructed, based on the given url. We send this message, and feed the resulting response_body data into the JSON parser using Json.from_string(). Then, we call the delegate with the received status code and the resulting Json.Node root node.

Note   This is a *blocking* network call, which should never be used in an event-driven UI program. Ideally, you should rather use the asynchronous libsoup API; however it resulted in a crash when I implemented this with Vala 0.44 and libsoup 2.66.2.

To wrap up, let's look at the application class NetRadio, which is contained in the file netRadio.vala, along with the POSIX main() function:

```
1   class NetRadio : Gtk.Application
2   {
3       public NetRadio()
4       {
5           Object( application_id: "de.vanille.valabook.
            NetRadio" );
6       }
7
```

```
8        protected override void activate()
9        {
10           var win = new MainWindow( this, "NetRadio -
             Streaming Internet Radio!" );
11           win.set_border_width( 10 );
12           win.set_default_size( 500, 800 );
13           win.show_all();
14       }
15   }
```

Our NetRadio application class derives from the generic GTK+ application class Gtk.Application.

This class handles GTK+ initialization, application uniqueness, and session management and provides some basic scriptability and desktop shell integration. Although Gtk.Application works fine with plain Gtk. Window instances, it is still recommended to use it together with Gtk. ApplicationWindow (which is the superclass of our MainWindow)—please refer to the GTK+ documentation for details.

Within an application class, the method activate() gets called when the initialization has been completed and the application is ready to set up the GUI. We create an instance of our MainWindow and configure a border width and a default window size:

```
1   int main (string[] args)
2   {
3       var app = new NetRadio();
4       var returnCode = app.run( args );
5       return returnCode;
6   }
```

Since Gtk.Application creates and configures the event loop on its own (you might want to compare this to the "Hello World" UI application in Chapter 3, where we did this manually), all we have to do is call its run() method. This method blocks until the event loop quits, afterward returning the POSIX return code.

Summary

We have introduced the basics for working with the graphical UI toolkit GTK+, presenting NetRadio as an example for a fully usable graphical Internet streaming radio application. The list of radio stations is accessed using a remote web service that has been written and is hosted by the author.

Note that we could only show the most relevant parts of the source code here. The full source code for this (and other) examples is available to readers on GitHub via the book's product page, located at www.apress.com/9781484253793.

CHAPTER 7

DBus

I was a lemon for a couple of weeks. I kept myself amused all that time by jumping in and out of a gin and tonic.

—Douglas Adams, The Hitchhiker's Guide to the Galaxy

This chapter covers DBus programming with Vala. After a brief overview about the core DBus concepts, we will show how to develop both a DBus client and a DBus server.

Introduction

A typical (UNIX) desktop environment, such as GNOME or KDE, is composed of many cooperating applications and services that allow users to complete their tasks.

Even a single application is sometimes distributed into multiple processes, for example, a backend (daemon) and a frontend (ui) process. These components usually have to communicate with each other using a shared protocol. For a long time, developers did this using the platform intrinsics, such as shared memory, message queues, pipes, or unix domain sockets.

© Michael Lauer 2019
M. Lauer, *Introducing Vala Programming*, https://doi.org/10.1007/978-1-4842-5380-9_7

With more and more applications being written specifically for one desktop environment, users have longed for a way to mix and match applications from different environments. To enable this, the freedesktop.org project has implemented DBus, an open *interprocess communication protocol (IPC)*, which was subsequently adopted by many projects as the definite communication standard—a leading role being taken by GNOME and KDE.

Nowadays, DBus has become the standard IPC on many UNIX-like platforms. Many applications have a DBus interface for controlling and/or scripting their behavior. Corresponding bindings are available for a lot of languages and environments, including `glib`—and thus, Vala.

Concepts

DBus is based on the client/server paradigm—servers are offering services that can be consumed by clients. There are two communication schemes, a *bidirectional* scheme for interactions with a request/response pattern and a *unidirectional* pattern offering a subscription service where parties can broadcast information to "interested" clients.

DBus implements a data bus system with an unlimited number of participants. Before being able to send and/or receive messages, a process needs to register with the bus. There is a central process (called dbus daemon) that provides the bus and the distribution of messages.

Although not mandatory, most UNIX-like multiuser platforms distinguish between a DBus *system bus* and a DBus *session bus*:

- **System Bus**: Only one system bus runs per machine. Access to services provided by the system bus is subject to matching authorization credentials.

- **Session Bus**: Every user session (as started by a login process) gets a dedicated session bus.

Before discussing the core concepts, let me introduce a helpful command-line tool for communicating with DBus: mdbus2. Take a moment to install this on your machine.

Bus Name The *bus name* is a bus-wide unique identification of any process communicating via DBus. There are *anonymous* and *well-known* bus names:

- **Anonymous** bus names consist of a colon (:) character, followed by a sequence of numbers and dots, for example, :12.123.

- **Well-Known** bus names can contain alphanumerical characters and dots. By default, reverse domain name notation is used, for example, org.freesmartphone. ogsmd.

When a process connects to the bus, it is assigned an anonymous bus name, called *unique connection name*. These names are never reused during the lifetime of the bus daemon—that is, you can be sure that a given name will always refer to the same application.

To offer services, a process may ask to own additional, well-known, bus names. Other applications can then use these services by sending messages to this bus name—without any knowledge about which process is actually owning that name.

You can call mdbus2 to list all bus names currently registered with DBus. Note that when run without -s, it queries the session bus.

On my machine (running a Linux Mint distribution), mdbus2 produces the following output:

```
1    $ mdbus2
2    com.canonical.indicator.application
3    com.canonical.indicator.sound
4    com.ubuntu.Upstart
5    org.PulseAudio1
```

```
6    org.a11y.Bus
7    org.freedesktop.DBus
8    org.freedesktop.Notifications
9    org.freedesktop.PowerManagement
10   org.freedesktop.network-manager-applet
11   org.freedesktop.secrets
12   org.freedesktop.thumbnails.Cache1
13   org.freedesktop.thumbnails.Manager1
14   org.freedesktop.thumbnails.Thumbnailer1
15   org.gnome.keyring
16   org.gtk.vfs.AfcVolumeMonitor
17   org.gtk.vfs.Daemon
18   org.gtk.vfs.GPhoto2VolumeMonitor
19   org.gtk.vfs.GoaVolumeMonitor
20   org.gtk.vfs.MTPVolumeMonitor
21   org.gtk.vfs.UDisks2VolumeMonitor
22   org.kde.StatusNotifierWatcher
23   org.pulseaudio.Server
24   org.xfce.FileManager
25   org.xfce.Panel
26   org.xfce.PowerManager
27   org.xfce.SessionManager
28   org.xfce.SettingsDaemon
29   org.xfce.Terminal5
30   org.xfce.Thunar
31   org.xfce.Xfconf
32   org.xfce.xfdesktop
```

Object Path Object paths are the communication addresses for DBus objects, which implement services. An object path starts with a slash (/) followed by number of path components containing alphanumerical characters separated with slashes, for example, /org/freesmartphone/phone/0.

Object paths look like file system pathnames and serve a similar purpose, that is, structuring the namespace. For any bus name, an unlimited number of objects (identified by their respective object path) can be registered.

You can use mdbus2 to list all object paths registered from a given bus name:

```
1    $ mdbus2 org.xfce.Terminal5
2    /
3    /org
4    /org/xfce
5    /org/xfce/Terminal
```

Interface An interface describes the communication syntax of a service. The communication flows via *method calls*, *properties*, and *signals*:

- **Method Calls** are point-to-point communication between two (not necessarily different) processes.

- **Properties** are variables exposed by a service. Their values can be accessed via getter and setter method calls.

- **Signals** are point-to-multipoint communication, initiated by one process and broadcasted to multiple other processes.

Method calls can have multiple parameters with the directions in, out, and inout. The access to properties can be restricted via qualifiers read, write, or readwrite. Signals can only have in parameters as there are no "return" values.

You can use mdbus2 to show the interfaces provided by an object:

```
1    $ mdbus2 org.xfce.Terminal5 /org/xfce/Terminal
2    [METHOD]    org.freedesktop.DBus.Properties.Get(s:interface_
                 name, s: property_name) -> (v:value)
```

3	[METHOD]	org.freedesktop.DBus.Properties. GetAll(s:interface_name) -> (a{sv}:properties)
4	[METHOD]	org.freedesktop.DBus.Properties.Set(s:interface_ name, s: property_name, v:value) -> ()
5	[SIGNAL]	org.freedesktop.DBus.Properties.Properties Changed(s: interface_name, a{sv}:changed_ properties, as:invalidated_properties)
6	[METHOD]	org.freedesktop.DBus.Introspectable.Introspect() -> (s: xml_data)
7	[METHOD]	org.freedesktop.DBus.Peer.Ping() -> ()
8	[METHOD]	org.freedesktop.DBus.Peer.GetMachineId() -> (s:machine_uuid)
9	[METHOD]	org.xfce.Terminal5.Launch(u:uid, ay:display- name, aay:argv) -> ()

Type System: Message and signal parameters adhere to a type system, in which values of various types are serialized into a sequence of bytes referred to as the standard *wire format*. Converting a value from some other representation into the wire format is called *marshaling*, and converting it back from the wire format is *unmarshaling*.

DBus knows a number of types which are mapped to the respective programming language's basic and compound types.

Error Handling: DBus has a simple way of error handling. Instead of successfully returning, a DBus method call can return an error message. Such an error message is textual and should indicate what happened. Error messages can contain alphanumerical characters, dots, and underscores—by convention they're using an inverse domain name address style. DBus itself defines a number of predefined system errors, such as org. freedesktop.DBus.Error.ServiceUnknown.

DBus in Vala

Support for DBus is implemented using the gio library. The part of gio that handles DBus is sometimes also called gdbus.[1] Vala contains support for writing DBus clients and DBus servers. We will show how to do both.

As a real-world example, we are going to extend NetRadio, our Internet streaming radio application from Chapter 6: Wouldn't it be helpful, if we could remotely control this application from another process, such as a command-line program? To make this happen, we will have to follow three steps:

1. Design a small interface that contains an API for browsing genres and stations, and toggle play/pause.

2. Write the methods implementing this interface and extend NetRadio with a DBus server listening to calls.

3. Write a command-line program that uses the DBus client API to communicate with NetRadio. Let's start with the design of the DBus interface.

DBus Interface

We will need to specify a bus name, a mount point for the service object, and method signatures. For the bus name and interface prefix, let's use de. vanille.NetRadio (inverse domain name notation, as recommended for DBus). The object path will be /.

---

[1]Prior to DBus support in gio, developers either used the (very low-level) freedesktop.org reference library libdbus or the (higher level) stand-alone dbus-glib binding library. Since the latter had many design problems that were exposed when DBus usage grew substantially, a rewrite was carried out in 2012. This rewrite has been called gdbus and is a part of gio since glib version 2.26.

To enable remote control for NetRadio, we will need the following methods:

- **ListGenres** shall return a list of genres with an id and a textual description, for each genre.

- **ListStations** shall return a list of stations, given a genre id. An error shall be issued when the genre id is unknown.

- **PlayStation** shall start streaming, given a genre id and a station id. An error shall be issued when the genre id or the station id is unknown, or when the station id is not valid for the given genre id.

- **Stop** shall stop streaming.

In DBus notation, a stands for an array, i for an integer, and s for a string. This leads to the following API:

```
1   de.vanille.NetRadio.ListGenres() -> a(is)
2   de.vanille.NetRadio.ListStations(i) -> a(is)
3   de.vanille.NetRadio.PlayStation(ii) -> ()
4   de.vanille.NetRadio.Stop() -> ()
```

To work with such an interface, DBus specifies a dedicated file format, called *DBus interface file*. A DBus interface file is an XML file describing one or more DBus interfaces. The format is standardized in the DBus specification and is supported by tools such as gdbus-codegen, and—more relevant for Vala—vala-dbus-binding-tool.

Here is the DBus interface file for our proposed API:

```
1   <!DOCTYPE node PUBLIC "-//freedesktop//DTD D-BUS Object
    Introspection 1.0//EN" "http://www.freedesktop.org/
    standards/dbus/1.0/introspect.dtd">
2   <node>
```

```
3      <interface name="de.vanille.NetRadio">
4        <method name="ListGenres">
5          <arg type="a(is)" direction="out"/>
6        </method>
7        <method name="ListStations">
8          <arg name="id" type="i" direction="in"/>
9          <arg type="a(is)" direction="out"/>
10       </method>
11       <method name="PlayStation">
12         <arg name="genre" type="i" direction="in"/>
13         <arg name="station" type="i" direction="in"/>
14       </method>
15       <method name="Stop">
16       </method>
17     </interface>
18     <fso:errordomain name="de.vanille.NetRadio" fso:no-
       container="true">
19     <error name="InvalidGenre">
20     </error>
21     <error name="InvalidStation">
22     </error>
23   </node>
```

Note   Unfortunately, the official DBus specification is lacking a
standard to provide errors in XML interface files; therefore we used
an extension here that has been proposed by the freesmartphone.org
project.

Example: DBus Server

To develop the DBus server, we need a Vala **interface** that resembles the DBus interface. The vala-dbus-binding-tool can read DBus XML interface files and construct the necessary .vala files for us; however we can also do it manually, as shown in the following.

Since we planned to return the genre and station lists with both a numerical id and a string, let's define a matching structure:

```
1   public struct Item
2   {
3       public int id;
4       public string name;
5   }
```

When encountering invalid genre or station ids, we would like to throw errors:

```
1   [DBus (name = "de.vanille.NetRadio")]
2   public errordomain NetRadioError
3   {
4       [DBus (name = "InvalidGenre")]
5       INVALID_GENRE,
6       [DBus (name = "InvalidStation")]
7       INVALID_STATION
8   }
```

This defines a custom error domain NetRadioError with two errors and provides the necessary DBus metadata (see discussion in the following) as code attributes. Now, consider the following interface:

```
1   [DBus (name = "de.vanille.NetRadio")]
2   public interface NetRadioDBusInterface : Object
3   {
```

```
4       [DBus (name = "ListGenres")]
5       public abstract async Item[] listGenres() throws
        DBusError, IOError ;
6
7       [DBus (name = "ListStations")]
8       public abstract async Item[] listStations( int id )
        throws NetRadioError, DBusError, IOError;
9
10      [DBus (name = "PlayStation")]
11      public abstract async void playStation( int genre, int
        station ) throws NetRadioError, DBusError, IOError;
12
13      [DBus (name = "Stop")]
14      public abstract async void stop() throws DBusError,
        IOError;
15   }
```

This looks pretty similar to a "normal" Vala interface—a notable difference being the [DBus (name=...)] code attributes, which augment the interface declaration with the necessary DBus metadata:

```
1   [DBus (name = "de.vanille.NetRadio")]
2   public interface NetRadioDBusInterface : Object
```

This sets up a DBus interface name for the Vala interface. Note that Vala DBus interfaces need to derive from GLib.Object. Although the DBus name and the interface name do not need to match, it makes sense to keep them similar:

```
1   [DBus (name = "ListGenres")]
2   public abstract async Item[] listGenres() throws DBusError,
    IOError;
```

This declares the DBus method name for the Vala method. Since we define an **interface** here, the method is declared as an **abstract** method. It is also an asynchronous method. Although you *can* define synchronous DBus interfaces, the DBus message processing is asynchronous by nature, due to the way DBus works. Asynchronous DBus interfaces are mapped to asynchronous Vala interfaces. They're more suitable for UI applications anyway, since they will not block the main loop.

The methods ListStations and PlayStation can fail with a domain-specific error. We thus have to specify our custom error domain NetRadioError and additionally two others, which are defined by glib. Although not yet enforced by Vala, it is important not to forget the two error domains DBusError and IOError:

1. A DBusError can be raised by the upper layers, such as DBusError.UNKNOWN_METHOD, when you call a non-registered method on a DBus object.

2. An IOError can be raised by the lower layers, such as when the DBus message bus daemon itself cannot be found.

Since DBus is interprocess communication, there are many ways for a method call to fail. Make sure to design domain-specific error domains in your DBus interfaces, and handle all errors in your DBus client code.

Note   Our Vala **interface** NetRadioDBusInterface is not only useful for the DBus server code. It is also helpful for writing a DBus client in Vala. Clients in other programming languages may directly use the DBus XML introspection file or use their custom tools to create code stubs.

To keep the DBus code separate from the rest of our application, we decide to implement the interface in a new controller class DBusServer:

```
1    const string NetRadioBusName = "de.vanille.NetRadio";
2    const string NetRadioPath = "/";
3
4    public class DBusServer : Object, NetRadioDBusInterface
5    {
6        private HashTable<string,StationModel> _knownStations;
7    }
```

After defining string constants for bus name and object path, we declare the DBusServer class inheriting from GLib.Object and NetRadioDbusInterface (see the preceding code). We hold a GLib. HashTable containing string keys and StationModel values, so that a station can be played by specifying a genre id and a station id:

```
1    public DBusServer()
2    {
3        _knownStations = new HashTable<string,StationModel>(
         str_hash, str_equal );
```

In the constructor, we create an instance of the hash table. Before moving on to the actual DBus interface, we need to make sure that a well-known bus name is registered:

```
1        Bus.own_name(
2            BusType.SESSION,
3            NetRadioBusName,
4            BusNameOwnerFlags.NONE,
5            onBusAcquired,
6            () => {},
7            () => warning( @"Could not acquire name
             $NetRadioBusName, the DBus interface will not be
             available!" )
8        );
9    }
```

In the constructor, we attempt to register the bus name by calling GLib.Bus.own_name(). This method takes the following six parameters:

1. GLib.BusType is the type of bus we connect to, SESSION for the session bus and SYSTEM for the system bus.

2. NetRadioBusName contains the well-known bus name we would like to register.

3. BusNameOwnerFlags allows tweaking the behavior in case someone else already owns or attempts to register the same name.

4. onBusAcquired is a delegate that is called, when a connection to the bus has been made.

5. Another delegate can be specified, when the well-known bus name has been successfully registered. We don't use this in our example; hence we supply an empty closure.

6. The last parameter is a delegate that gets called, if we can't register the well-known bus name.

We just show a warning here:

```
1   void onBusAcquired( DBusConnection conn )
2   {
3       try
4       {
5           conn.register_object<NetRadioDBusInterface>(
            NetRadioPath, this );
6       }
7       catch ( IOError e )
8       {
```

```
9            error( @"Could not acquire path $NetRadioPath:
             $(e.message)" );
10       }
11       print( @"DBus Server is now listening on
         $NetRadioBusName $NetRadioPath...\n" );
12   }
```

This method gets called after a connection with the bus has been established. We attempt to register our service on the NetRadioPath. In addition to the desired object path and the actual instance that becomes the service object (i.e., handles the method calls), the method register_object() takes a generic parameter containing an interface name— NetRadioDBusInterface in our case.

Like many DBus operations, register_object() can fail; hence it's very important to handle errors like the GLib.IOError in this case.

Note   Object path registration and registering a well-known bus name do not depend on each other. Since every DBus participant gets at least one name, registering an object path may succeed, even when registering an (additional) well-known bus name fails.

Before implementing the DBus interface, let's change one thing in the previously written controller classes DirectoryClient and PlayerController. The DBus interface implementation calls methods on the controller classes. For this, it needs references to both of them. In the previous chapter, the MainWindow held an instance of the PlayerController, which itself held an instance of the DirectoryClient.

Since our class DBusServer will also need references to these, we could either create additional instances or find a way to reuse the existing ones. At least for the PlayerController, it does not make sense to create more than just one, since we only have one audio output and are not interested in a cacophony with multiple streams playing concurrently.

Therefore, it might be useful to design each controller class as a *singleton*. A singleton is an object-oriented architectural pattern that ensures that only one instance of a class gets ever created, and provides a central way of accessing this instance. Implementing a singleton in Vala is simple:[2]

```
1    public class SomeClass : Object
2    {
3        private static SomeClass __instance;
4
5        private SomeClass() { ... };
6
7        public static sharedInstance()
8        {
9            if ( __instance == null )
10           {
11               __instance = new SomeClass();
12           }
13           return __instance;
14       }
15   }
```

To make sure that only one instance is ever created, we declare the constructor **private** and create a member variable that will hold our shared instance. The static method sharedInstance() then checks whether the one-and-only instance has already been created. Like this, everyone can use SomeClass.sharedInstance() to get a reference to the singleton. Note that this has been done for both the PlayerController and the DirectoryClient.

---

[2]While this is an instructive example, note that GObject-based classes have built-in singleton support. Vala provides this via the [SingleInstance] decorator.

Let's implement the actual DBus interface now—we need to write code for the methods listGenres (), listStations(), playStation(), and stop():

```
1  public async Item[] listGenres() throws DBusError, IOError
2  {
3      var genres = yield DirectoryClient.sharedInstance().
       loadGenres();
4      var items = new Item[genres.length] {};
5      for ( int i = 0; i < genres.length; ++i )
6      {
7          items[i] = Item() { id = i, name = genres[i].title };
8      }
9      return items;
10 }
```

Here, we call the (asynchronous) loadGenres() on the shared instance of the DirectoryClient using yield, which will temporarily suspend the execution of this method until the result is available.

In alignment with our defined interface, we do not want to return full GenreModel objects via DBus but rather create an array of Item structures to hold an index and the respective genre title:

```
1  public async Item[] listStations( int id ) throws
   NetRadioError, DBusError, IOError
2  {
3      var genre = new GenreModel( id );
4      var stations = yield DirectoryClient.sharedInstance().
       loadStations( genre );
5      if ( stations == null )
6      {
7          throw new NetRadioError.INVALID_GENRE( @"Genre id
           $id is invalid" );
```

```
8        }
9        var items = new Item[stations.length] {};
10       for ( int i = 0; i < stations.length; ++i )
11       {
12           var station = stations[i];
13           var key = @"$id.$i";
14           _knownStations[key] = station;
15           items[i] = Item() { id = i, name = station.name };
16       }
17       return items;
18   }
```

The method listStations() is pretty similar; however, as we iterate through the stations received from the DirectoryClient, we store the known stations in our _knownStations hash table. The DirectoryClient's loadStations() does not take a genre id but rather an instance of a GenreModel though, so we have to create this beforehand.

If we don't get a valid array of stations from the DirectoryClient, the provided genre id must[3] have been invalid; hence we **throw** our error NetRadioError.INVALID_GENRE here:

```
1    public async void playStation( int genre, int station )
     throws NetRadioError, DBusError, IOError
2    {
3        var key = @"$genre.$station";
4        var theStation = _knownStations[key];
5        if ( theStation != null )
6        {
```

---

[3]Actually, even given a valid genre id, there *might* be a whole lot of other errors, since we're hitting the network here. Production-ready code should do better, e.g., by inspecting the HTTP status code and throwing appropriate errors in the DirectoryClient.

```
 7            PlayerController.sharedInstance().playStation
              ( theStation );
 8        }
 9        else
10        {
11            throw new NetRadioError.INVALID_STATION( @"Can't
              find a station for genre id $genre and station id
              $station" );
12        }
13    }
```

We attempt to look up the requested StationModel object by genre and station id in our hash table _knownStations. If we find a station, we hand it over to the DirectoryClient. If there is no station, we raise the a NetRadioError.

Now, with the DBusServer being implemented, we need to instantiate this object. A good place to do so is in the main program netRadio.vala—right after the creation of our MainWindow class in activate():

```
1    protected override void activate()
2    {
3        Gtk.ApplicationWindow window = new MainWindow( this,
         "NetRadio - Streaming Internet Radio!" );
4        window.set_border_width( 10 );
5        window.set_default_size( 500, 800 );
6        window.show_all();
7
8        new DBusServer();
9    }
```

This concludes our work on the DBus server.

Let's test this server before writing a dedicated client to talk to it. Again, we can do this with mdbus2:

```
1    $ mdbus2 de.vanille.NetRadio
2    /
3    /de
4    /de/vanille
5    /de/vanille/valabook
6    /de/vanille/valabook/NetRadio
7    /de/vanille/valabook/NetRadio/window
8    /de/vanille/valabook/NetRadio/window/1
```

You probably didn't expect to see that many object paths here—this is due to GTK+ registering an object path for every instantiated Gtk. ApplicationWindow, where it provides basic scripting capabilities. For now, we are only interested in everything that is provided by the root node "/", since this is the location where we have registered our object implementing the interface de.vanille. NetRadio. Listing the available object paths for the root node:

```
1    $ mdbus2 org.vanille.NetRadio /
2    [METHOD]    org.freedesktop.DBus.Properties.Get(s:interface_
                 name, s: property_name) -> (v:value)
3    [METHOD]    org.freedesktop.DBus.Properties.
                 GetAll(s:interface_name) -> (a{sv}:properties)
4    [METHOD]    org.freedesktop.DBus.Properties.Set(s:interface_
                 name, s: property_name, v:value) -> ()
5    [SIGNAL]    org.freedesktop.DBus.Properties.Properties
                 Changed(s: interface_name, a{sv}:changed_
                 properties, as:invalidated_properties)
```

```
6    [METHOD]    org.freedesktop.DBus.Introspectable.
                 Introspect() -> (s: xml_data)
7    [METHOD]    org.freedesktop.DBus.Peer.Ping() -> ()
8    [METHOD]    org.freedesktop.DBus.Peer.GetMachineId() ->
                 (s:machine_uuid)
9    [METHOD]    de.vanille.NetRadio.ListGenres() ->
                 (a(is):result)
10   [METHOD]    de.vanille.NetRadio.ListStations(i:id) ->
                 (a(is):result)
11   [METHOD]    de.vanille.NetRadio.PlayStation(i:genre,
                 i:station) -> ()
12   [METHOD]    de.vanille.NetRadio.Stop() -> ()
```

Again, slightly more than expected: Any method or signal with an
org.freedesktop.DBus prefix is part of a standard (meta-)interface,
implemented by DBus for every object on the bus. Fortunately, our de.
vanille.NetRadio interface is present as well:

```
1    $ mdbus2 de.vanille.NetRadio / de.vanille.NetRadio.
     ListGenres
2    ([(0, 'Adult Contemporary'), (1, 'Classical'), (2,
     'Country'), (3, 'Decades'), (4, 'Electronic'), (5, 'Folk'),
     (6, 'International'), (7, 'Jazz'), (8, 'Misc'), (9, 'Pop'),
     (10, 'R&B/Urban'), (11, 'Rap'), (12, 'Reggae'), (13,
     'Rock'), (14, 'Talk & Speech')],)
```

Listing the genres works.

```
1    $ mdbus2 de.vanille.NetRadio / de.vanille.NetRadio.
     ListStations 4
```

```
2   ([(0, 'Radio Kontho'), (1, 'Славянский Мир'), (2, 'Art
    Bell Classics'), (3, 'Buena Vibra Radio'), (4, 'Of Service
    To Others Network'), (5, 'Radio Brocken Kinderzeit'),
    (6, 'Dala FM Kano'), (7, 'Freedom Radio'), (8, 'Muallim
    Radio'), (9, 'Anika Radio'), (10, 'Path Radio'), (11, 'Red
    Rose Fm'), (12, 'Radio Biafra International'), (13, 'Sawt
    Al Mustaqbal'), (14, 'BBS Radio'), (15, 'Remix Radio'),
    (16, 'Garkuwa FM 95.5 Sokoto'), (17, 'Pulse Talk Radio'),
    (18, 'Route 66 Radio'), (19, 'Idiot Radio Network')],)
```

Listing the stations for a valid genre works as well. Let's provoke an error by providing an invalid genre id:

```
1   $ mdbus2 de.vanille.NetRadio / de.vanille.NetRadio.
    PlayStation 99 3
2   [ERR]: GDBus.Error:de.vanille.NetRadio.InvalidStation: No
    station found with genre id 99 and station id 3
```

Last but not least, let's try playing a station:

```
1   $ mdbus2 de.vanille.NetRadio / de.vanille.NetRadio.
    PlayStation 4 0
2   ()
```

The call returns the expected (successful) empty response and starts the stream (I hear it playing, trust me on that).

Example: DBus Client

To keep it simple, we will implement a small command-line application that allows us to list genres, list stations, play, and pause.

Writing a DBus client in Vala is straightforward: First, you need to get a proxy object that implements the desired interface from the dbus daemon. Afterward, every method call on the interface is transformed into an actual DBus message. This includes error handling, emitting signals, and querying properties:

```
1    MainLoop loop;
2
3    public class NetRadioClient : Object
4    {
5        NetRadioDBusInterface netRadioServerProxy;
6    }
```

Although this application is not a UI application, we will use asynchronous methods, which are not going to work unless we have a main loop.

The class NetRadioClient derives from GLib.Object and has the interface proxy NetRadioDBusInterface as a private member variable. In order to populate this proxy object, we need to talk to the dbus daemon. We could do this in a constructor; however it is preferable to implement a dedicated method for that, since constructors should not fail or throw errors:

```
1    public bool init()
2    {
3        try
4        {
5            netRadioServerProxy = Bus.get_proxy_sync(
6                BusType.SESSION,
7                "org.vanille.NetRadio",
8                "/" );
9        }
10       catch ( IOError e )
```

```
11          {
12                  print( @"Could not create proxy: $(e.message)" );
13                  return false;
14          }
15
16          return true;
17      }
```

As part of the initialization, we try to get the proxy object from GLib.
Bus. This is possible in either a synchronous or an asynchronous way. For
simplicity, we're using the synchronous interface get_proxy_sync() here.
This method needs to know the proxy's bus type, bus name, and object
path. Always remember: Every DBus operation can fail; hence we need to
handle all potential errors.

Our public API for this class will contain four methods:

1. listGenres()

2. listStations(**int** genre)

3. playStation(**int** genre, **int** station)

4. stop()

We prefer to write asynchronous methods, since we also have defined
asynchronous DBus methods in the interface NetRadioDBusInterface:

```
1   public async void listGenres()
2   {
3       try
4       {
5           var items = yield netRadioServerProxy.listGenres();
6           foreach ( var item in items )
7           {
8               print( "%03d: %s\n", item.id, item.name );
9           }
```

```
10      }
11      catch ( Error e )
12      {
13          print( @"Could not list genres: $(e.message)" );
14      }
15      loop.quit();
16  }
```

To get the list of genres, we call the DBus method listGenres(). We then print it line by line. After the method has completed, we instruct the main loop to quit. Note the error handling:

```
1   public async void listStations( int genre )
2   {
3       try
4       {
5           var items = yield netRadioServerProxy.
            listStations( genre );
6           foreach ( var item in items )
7           {
8               print( "%03d: %s\n", item.id, item.name );
9           }
10      }
11      catch ( Error e )
12      {
13          print( @"Could not list stations: $(e.message)" );
14      }
15      loop.quit();
16  }
```

Listing the stations works similarly, although we have to provide a genre id:

```
1    public async void playStation( int genre, int station )
2    {
3        try
4        {
5            yield netRadioServerProxy.playStation( genre,
             station );
6        }
7        catch ( Error e )
8        {
9            print( @"Could not play station: $(e.message)" );
10       }
11       loop.quit();
12   }
```

No surprises when playing a station.

```
1    public async void stop()
2    {
3        try
4        {
5            yield netRadioServerProxy.stop();
6        }
7        catch ( Error e )
8        {
9            print( @"Could not stop: $(e.message)" );
10       }
11       loop.quit();
12   }
```

And the same for stopping.

Let's move on to the main() function now:

```
1   int main( string[] args )
2   {
3       var client = new NetRadioClient();
4       if ( !client.init() )
5       {
6           return -1;
7       }
8
9       if ( args.length < 2 )
10      {
11          print( "Usage: %s <command> [param] [param]\n",
            args[0] );
12          return -1;
13      }
```

After instantiating the class we have just written, we call init() to find out whether initialization succeeded. If there is an error (such as, no DBus server implementing the desired interface, or DBus not being available at all), we will return the POSIX error code -1:

```
1       switch ( args[1] )
2       {
3           case "lg":
4               client.listGenres();
5               break;
6
7           case "ls":
8               var genre = int.parse( args[2] );
9               client.listStations( genre );
10              break;
11
```

```
12              case "play":
13                  var genre = int.parse( args[2] );
14                  var station = int.parse( args[3] );
15                  client.playStation( genre, station );
16                  break;
17
18              case "stop":
19                  client.stop();
20                  break;
21
22              default:
23                  print( "Unknown command: %s\n", args[1] );
24                  break;
25          }
```

We inspect the command-line arguments and decide which method to call. Note that in this case, we are calling an asynchronous method from within a synchronous one. At this point in time, the main loop is not running yet. This means that the method call only schedules the method to run "later" (i.e., once the main loop has been started):

```
1       loop = new MainLoop();
2       loop.run();
3
4       return 0;
5   }
```

Last but not least, the MainLoop is instantiated and run.

Before test driving our new DBus NetRadio client, remember to start the UI application, since the latter is also our DBus server. Otherwise, get_proxy_sync() will raise an error:

```
1   $ ./netradio-client lg
2   000: Adult Contemporary
```

198

```
3    001: Classical
4    002: Country
5    003: Decades
6    004: Electronic
7    005: Folk
8    006: International
9    007: Jazz
10   008: Misc
11   009: Pop
12   010: R&B/Urban
13   011: Rap
14   012: Reggae
15   013: Rock
16   014: Talk & Speech
```

Listing the primary genres works fine. Let's choose to see all stations belonging to the genre "Electronic," which has the genre id 4:

```
1    $ ./netradio-client ls 4
2    000: Radio Kontho
3    001: SOMA.FM: Space Station Soma
4    002: Art Bell Classics
5    003: Buena Vibra Radio
6    004: Of Service To Others Network
7    005: Radio Brocken Kinderzeit
8    006: Dala FM Kano
9    007: Freedom Radio
10   008: Muallim Radio
11   009: Anika Radio
12   010: Path Radio
13   011: Red Rose Fm
14   012: Radio Biafra International
```

```
15    013: Sawt Al Mustaqbal
16    014: BBS Radio
17    015: Remix Radio
18    016: Garkuwa FM 95.5 Sokoto
19    017: Pulse Talk Radio
20    018: Route 66 Radio
21    019: Idiot Radio Network
```

Works as expected. To wrap up, let's try playing and pausing:

```
1    $ ./netradio-client play 4 5     # music is now playing
2    $ ./netradio-client stop         # music will now stop
```

Summary

We have introduced the interprocess communication standard DBus and learned how to design a DBus interface. We used Vala to write a DBus server and a DBus client. We also learned to use mdbus2, a powerful tool to introspect running DBus server process and to communicate with them.

CHAPTER 8

Linux

In those days spirits were brave, the stakes were high, men were real men, women were real women and small furry creatures from Alpha Centauri were real small furry creatures from Alpha Centauri.

—Douglas Adams, The Hitchhiker's Guide to the Galaxy

This chapter shows how to use Vala for writing code that accesses platform-specific Linux low-level features.

Introduction

Linux is an operating system kernel. The initial implementation has been written by Linus Torvalds in 1991. Since then it has not only become one of the most successful open source community projects ever but also the most widespread operating system kernel. This is mainly due to Google's Android smartphone operating system using a kernel derived from Linux. Linux is powering billions (> 1.000.000.000) of devices, thus, probably one of yours, too.

© Michael Lauer 2019
M. Lauer, *Introducing Vala Programming*, https://doi.org/10.1007/978-1-4842-5380-9_8

Many of the Vala features are independent of the actual platform, since it runs on any platform that has `glib` available. With the full support for UI toolkits, such as GTK+, Vala is a good choice for writing graphical desktop applications. It is, however, also extremely suitable for lower level programming. We have already seen a glimpse of that in Chapter 5.

linux.vapi

The file `linux.vapi` contains a large number of constants and functions wrapping specific features of the Linux operating system, such as

- Raw console programming (`linux/kd.h`)

- EventFd (`linux/eventfd.h`)

- Epoll (`sys/epoll.h`)

- Framebuffer (`linux/fb.h`)

- GSM Multiplexing (`linux/gsmmux.h`)

- I2C and SPI

- INotify (`sys/inotify.h`)

- RFKill (`linux/rfkill.h`)

- SignalFd (`linux/signalfd.h`)

- Networking and NetLink

- Input subsystem (`linux/input.h`)

- RTC (`linux/rtc.h`)

- Terminal I/O and Virtual Terminal (`linux/vt.h`)

- Wireless Extensions (WEXT)

- And more

It also includes a number of non-POSIX extensions to facilities defined by POSIX. These are largely implemented in the standard C library `glibc`. One would assume that those reside in a corresponding file called `glibc.vapi`— for historical reasons though, they are instead defined in `linux.vapi`.

There are a lot of kernel features worthwhile to discuss. The one I picked as an example is file notification.

File Notification

Many applications that deal with documents, such as a text editor, have a way to automatically reload a document when its contents changes "behind the back" of the application.

There is no common or standardized way to monitor files on various operating systems; thus, this feature has to be implemented in a platform-specific manner. As an example for that, we will write a command-line application for Linux which, once executed, waits until a change in a file occurs.

The mechanism behind this is a kernel-provided interface, called *inotify*:

- `inotify_init()` initializes the inotify subsystem and returns a file descriptor for reading.

- `inotify_add_watch()` schedules a file system path to be observed for events. You can define which kind of file events to watch for, for example, simply accessing the file, modifying, removing, and so on.

- `inotify_rm_watch()` removes a file system path from the list of paths to be observed.

Whenever the inotify subsystem gets triggered (by someone performing an action on a watched path), the kernel writes a structure to the file descriptor that contains the access details. In the file linux. vapi, there are bindings for this API.

Example: inotifyWatcher

We create a class Watcher that encapsulates the necessary actions:

```
1   public class Watcher : Object
2   {
3       private int _fd;
4       private uint _watch;
5       private IOChannel _channel;
6       private uint8[] _buffer;
7
8       const uint BUFFER_LENGTH = 4096;
9   }
```

The class contains a few member variables to hold our state, in particular one for the inotify subsystem file descriptor (_fd), as well as a _buffer to hold the kernel notification structure and a GLib. IOChannel: This is the abstraction of a main loop event source.

Note   Of course, we could use the low-level functions select(2) or poll(2) here; however these are blocking calls which can't be used in a scenario where we have a GLib.MainLoop running (consider the previously mentioned UI application that allows to edit a document). Therefore, we rather add an arbitrary file descriptor as an additional event source to the glib main loop.

```
1    public Watcher( string path, Linux.InotifyMaskFlags mask )
2    {
3        _buffer = new uint8[BUFFER_LENGTH];
```

The constructor takes a `string` path to a file to watch for and a `Linux.InotifyMaskFlags` parameter specifying which kind of actions to react to.

First, we allocate the `_buffer` that is later used for receiving the kernel notification structure:

```
1        _fd = Linux.inotify_init();
2        if ( _fd < 0 )
3        {
4            error( @"Can't initialize the inotify subsystem:
             $(strerror(errno))" );
5        }
```

We initialize the inotify subsystem and store the resulting file descriptor. Similar to many POSIX functions, `inotify_init()` returns a negative value, if there was a problem:

```
1        _channel = new IOChannel.unix_new( _fd );
2        _watch = _channel.add_watch( IOCondition.IN |
             IOCondition.HUP, onActionFromInotify );
```

We wrap the file descriptor in a `GLib.IOChannel` and add it to the main loop by calling `add_watch ()`. This call takes a `GLib.IOCondition` mask and a callback. In our case, we are interested in two conditions:

1. `IOCondition.IN` means that our callback will be called when the given `IOChannel` (hence our file descriptor) is ready for reading.

2. `IOCondition.HUP` results in our callback being called when the given `IOChannel` encounters a hangup (error) situation.

If at least one of these conditions is true, the glib main loop will schedule a call to onActionFromInotify():

```
1      var ok = Linux.inotify_add_watch( _fd, path, mask );
2      if ( ok == -1 )
3      {
4          error( @"Can't watch $path: $(strerror(errno))" );
5      }
6      print( @"Watching $path...\n" );
7  }
```

We now register the file system path to watch for with the inotify subsystem. inotify_add_watch () takes the stored file descriptor, the path to watch, and a mask specifying which actions the kernel should watch for.

Let's take a closer look at the aforementioned callback now. This receives the source and the condition that occurred as parameters:

```
1  protected bool onActionFromInotify( IOChannel source,
   IOCondition condition )
2  {
3      if ( ( condition & IOCondition.HUP ) == IOCondition.HUP )
4      {
5          error( @"Received HUP from inotify, can't get any
           more updates" );
6          Posix.exit( -1 );
7      }
```

Since GLib.IOCondition is a mask, several IOCondition flags may be OR-ed together. If IOCondition.HUP is part of the mask, we print an error and exit() the program with a negative return code:

```
1      if ( ( condition & IOCondition.IN ) == IOCondition.IN )
2      {
3          var bytesRead = Posix.read( _fd, _buffer, BUFFER_
           LENGTH );
```

```
4          Linux.InotifyEvent* pevent = (Linux.InotifyEvent*)
           _buffer;
5          handleEvent( *pevent );
6      }
```

If IOCondition.IN is part of the mask, we read() the kernel structure from the file descriptor _fd and cast the raw bytes to a Linux.InotifyEvent structure. We then call our helper method handleEvent() to deal with the details of the event.

```
1      return true;
2  }
```

By convention, the Glib.IOChannel expects the callback to return a boolean value that instructs the main loop whether to continue (**true**) calling it for such actions or whether to remove (**false**) the source from the main loop:

```
1  protected void handleEvent( Linux.InotifyEvent event )
2  {
3      print( "BOOM!\n" );
4      Posix.exit( 0 );
5  }
```

Instead of a simple printout, we could add code for further inspection of the Linux.InotifyEvent kernel structure here. This would show us the exact reasons why we have been called. In our case though, we just want the program to return with the positive return code 0:

```
1  ~Watcher()
2  {
3      if ( _watch != 0 )
4      {
5          Source.remove( _watch );
6      }
```

```
 7        if ( _fd != -1 )
 8        {
 9            Posix.close( _fd );
10        }
11   }
```

Although not really necessary in this example (since the kernel will clean up all resources when a process exists), it is always a good practice to clean up. In this case, we remove our GLib.Source from the main loop and close() our file descriptor:

```
1    int main( string[] args )
2    {
3        var watcher = new Watcher( "/tmp/foo.txt",
         Linux.InotifyMaskFlags. ACCESS );
4        var loop = new MainLoop();
5        loop.run();
6        return 0;
7    }
```

The main() function creates a Watcher for the file /tmp/foo.txt, then instantiates a GLib. MainLoop, and runs it.

To see how this program works, you need two command-line terminals. In one terminal, create the file to watch for, and then execute our example:

```
1    $ echo "This is the content of foo.txt" > /tmp/foo.txt
2    $ vala --pkg=linux inotifyWatcher.watcher
3    Watching /tmp/foo.txt...
```

In the other terminal, trigger the inotify watcher by reading the contents of the watched file:

```
1    $ cat /tmp/foo.txt
2    This is the content of foo.txt
```

If everything worked, the first terminal should now contain

```
1   $ vala --pkg=linux inotifyWatcher.watcher
2   Watching /tmp/foo.txt...
3   BOOM!
```

Summary

We have introduced the platform-specific linux.vapi, which contains bindings to various low-level features of the Linux operating system. As an example, we presented a file monitor that implements watching for file access using the Linux inotify subsystem.

CHAPTER 9

External Libraries

A towel is about the most massively useful thing an interstellar hitchhiker can have. Partly it has great practical value. You can wrap it around you for warmth as you bound across the cold moons of Jaglan Beta; you can lie on it on the brilliant marble-sanded beaches of Santraginus V, inhaling the heady sea vapors; you can sleep under it beneath the stars which shine so redly on the desert world of Kakrafoon; use it to sail a miniraft down the slow heavy River Moth; wet it for use in hand-to-hand-combat; wrap it round your head to ward off noxious fumes or avoid the gaze of the Ravenous Bugblatter Beast of Traal (such a mind-boggingly stupid animal, it assumes that if you can't see it, it can't see you); you can wave your towel in emergencies as a distress signal, and of course dry yourself off with it if it still seems to be clean enough.

—Douglas Adams, The Hitchhiker's Guide to the Galaxy

This chapter shows how to use the functionality provided by external libraries from Vala programs, that is, how to write binding files for C APIs.

© Michael Lauer 2019
M. Lauer, *Introducing Vala Programming*, https://doi.org/10.1007/978-1-4842-5380-9_9

Bindings

One of the most notable strengths of Vala is the straightforward way to use existing functionality, provided it is exposed via a C API. This holds both for C source code directly embedded in your project as well as for (external) libraries. The process is the same in either case; hence for the remainder of this chapter, we will only discuss external libraries.

In contrast to most other programming languages, Vala does not need any run-time facilities to integrate C libraries: Everything is done at compile time. Nevertheless, we use the common term *binding* when referring to an external library from Vala—however, keep in mind that the necessary glue is just declarative and very lightweight.

To generate a binding for a library, you need to write a `.vapi` file, which informs Vala of the constants, global variables, functions, and structures typically found in the corresponding `.h` header file. Although Vala cannot directly use C header files, creating VAPI declarations is very simple.

It makes an important difference though, whether the chosen library is based on the `glib` object system or not. For libraries based on `GObject`, there is an automated process to create a VAPI. For all other libraries, you have to create the VAPI manually.

We will explain both cases. Let's start by binding an external library that is not based on `GObject`.

Warning   Binding a C library is a challenging task. If something is not fully correct in the VAPI, chances are that you might get C compilation errors and/or crashes at run-time. Don't get frustrated, it's a great learning experience.

Example: Binding libxmp

libxmp is a small library created for XMP, a multimedia audio player, designed to play *modules*. A module is a music file format that has been created in the 1990s for the Commodore AMIGA.

Notable tasks of libxmp are parsing the module format and rendering audio buffers. libxmp does not already come with a Vala binding.

Note   When manually writing a VAPI, it is preferable to have some experience in using the library from C. Make sure to always consult the header file and the official documentation.

We will not *completely* bind libxmp; this could fit in a book on its own. We will concentrate on some key areas though.

To start, create a new file libxmp.vapi and save it in a directory that will also contain the example program. Remember that VAPI files are just Vala files with an emphasis on declarative statements. As such, they have to contain valid Vala syntax.

It is good practice to put all the functionality of an external library in a dedicated namespace; hence we start with the following:

```
1   [CCode (cprefix="XMP_", lower_case_cprefix="xmp_",
        cheader_filename=" xmp.h")]
2   namespace Xmp
3   {
4   }
```

The first line contains the three CCode attributes cprefix, lower_case_cprefix, and cheader_filename:

1. cprefix specifies a prefix that can be added to namespace, struct, and **class** declarations. It will be applied to all entities without a dedicated cname in that scope.

2. lower_case_cprefix tells Vala to add that prefix to all other declarations.

3. cheader_filename defines the C header file to #include whenever an entity of the enclosing scope is referred to.

Step 1

As the first step, we want to print out the library's version string and version code. In the header file xmp.h, we can find the following lines:

```
1    EXPORT extern const char *xmp_version;
2    EXPORT extern const unsigned int xmp_vercode;
```

We can safely ignore the EXPORT part, which just refers to a macro that abstracts the compiler- specific syntax to export library symbols. The interesting parts are **const char*** xmp_version and unsigned **int** xmp_vercode, which we map to a **const** string and a **const** uint, respectively. We thus insert the following snippet within the namespace declaration:

```
1    [CCode (cname = "xmp_version")]
2    public const string version;
3    [CCode (cname = "xmp_vercode")]
4    public const uint vercode;
```

Note   Unfortunately, whenever Vala sees a **const** entity declared in a VAPI, it derives an all-uppercase C name by default, in this case XMP_version, respectively, XMP_vercode. For libxmp, this does not fit, as they're called differently. Hence, we have to override this default using a dedicated cname code attribute. As a general note for conceiving bindings, always aim for a reasonable balance between the original API and Vala conventions. While it usually might be preferable to stick rather close to the names in the C API—to prevent alienating those developers who have already used the library from C—following the Vala conventions makes an API more *natural* to use. In this particular case, it might have been more appropriate to rename the constants to VERSION and VERCODE—following the "all uppercase names for constants" convention in Vala.

Let's test our VAPI by writing the following code to a file called xmptest.vala:

```
1   int main( string[] args )
2   {
3       print( "Using XMP version %s (%u)\n", Xmp.version,
        Xmp.vercode );
4       return 0;
5   }
```

When compiling, we need to tell Vala that it should include the declarations we just wrote in libxmp.vapi:

```
1   $ valac -o xmptest --pkg=libxmp --vapidir=. xmptest.vala
```

We have already used the --pkg command-line argument to add external libraries before. Note that you can use --vapidir to add a VAPI search directory. This is required for custom VAPI files (or if you want to override any of the VAPI files that come with the Vala compiler). Running xmptest on my machine produces the following output:

```
1    $ ./xmptest
2    Using XMP version 4.4.1 (263169)
```

Step 2

For this step, we are going to bind xmp_get_format_list(), which returns the list of module formats understood by libxmp. This is defined in xmp.h as follows:

```
1    EXPORT char **xmp_get_format_list(void);
```

A pointer to a pointer of **char** looks like we could map this as a string[] in Vala. We thus add the following to our VAPI:

```
1    public string[] get_format_list();
```

We attempt to use this function from within the main() function in xmptest.vala as follows:

```
1    foreach ( var format in Xmp.get_format_list() )
2    {
3        print( "XMP recognizes format '%s'\n", format );
4    }
```

Compiling the example now leads to an unexpected error in the generated C code:

```
1   xmptest.c:25:32: error: too many arguments to function
    call, expected 0, have 1
2              _tmp1_ = xmp_get_format_list (&_tmp0_);
3              ~~~~~~~~~~~~~~~~~~~~~~   ^~~~~~~
4   /usr/local/include/xmp.h:330:1: note: 'xmp_get_format_
    list' declared here
5   EXPORT char      **xmp_get_format_list (void);
6   ^
7   /usr/local/include/xmp.h:23:17: note: expanded from macro
    'EXPORT'
8   #define EXPORT __attribute__ ((visibility ("default")))
9                   ^
10  1 error generated.
11  error: cc exited with status 256
12  Compilation failed: 1 error(s), 0 warning(s)
```

Ignoring the EXPORT noise, it looks like Vala has transformed the call to get_format_list() into the following line:

```
1   _tmp1_ = xmp_get_format_list (&_tmp0_);
```

We can observe an additional parameter (&_tmp0_), which is unexpected and wrong, since xmp_get_format_list() does not take any parameters. This parameter has been added because of the way Vala handles arrays: By default, whenever a Vala array is used as a parameter, it gets transformed to C code transferring two parameters: one holding a pointer to the elements and one for the number of elements contained in the array. Since our function is supposed to return an array of strings, Vala assumes the number of elements is returned as well.

217

Consulting the respective libxmp documentation, we can find the following specification for the return parameter of xmp_get_format_list():

> "A NULL-terminated array of strings containing the names of all supported module formats."

For cases like this, Vala supports the boolean CCode attribute array_null_terminated. Changing the VAPI correspondingly leads to a successful compilation:

```
1  [CCode (array_null_terminated = true)]
2  public string[] get_format_list();
```

We can now run xmptest, which results in something similar to the following (truncated) output:

```
1   $ ./xmptest
2   Using XMP version 4.4.1 (263169)
3   XMP recognizes format 'Fast Tracker II'
4   XMP recognizes format 'Amiga Protracker/Compatible'
5   XMP recognizes format 'Startrekker'
6   XMP recognizes format 'Soundtracker'
7   [...]
8   XMP recognizes format 'Titanics Player'
9   xmptest(37464,0x7fff8f7ec340) malloc: *** error for object
    0x107dc98a9: pointer being freed was not allocated
10  *** set a breakpoint in malloc_error_break to debug
11  [1]    37464 abort      ./xmptest
```

While most of the output looks good, we still get an unexpected runtime error when the program terminates—a memory block gets released ("freed") that wasn't supposed to. The error message does not tell us where exactly the problem happened, so let's run the program in a debugger to get a backtrace:

```
1    (lldb) bt
2    * thread #1, queue = 'com.apple.main-thread',
     stop reason = signal SIGABRT
3      * frame #0: 0x00007fff56c04e3e libsystem_kernel.dylib`
                   pthread_kill + 10
4        frame #1: 0x00007fff56d43150 libsystem_pthread.
                   dylib`pthread_kill + 333
5        frame #2: 0x00007fff56b61312 libsystem_c.dylib
                   `abort + 127
6        frame #3: 0x00007fff56c5e866 libsystem_malloc.
                   dylib`free + 521
7        frame #4: 0x0000000100000f11 xmptest`_vala_array_
                   destroy + 97
8        frame #5: 0x0000000100000e63 xmptest`_vala_array_
                   free + 35
9        frame #6: 0x0000000100000dd3 xmptest`_vala_main + 275
10       frame #7: 0x0000000100000ea2 xmptest`main + 34
11       frame #8: 0x00007fff56ab5115 libdyld.dylib`start + 1
12       frame #9: 0x00007fff56ab5115 libdyld.dylib`start + 1
```

The offending part is contained in frame #4, namely, _vala_array_ destroy(). This is a helper function created by Vala for an array of pointers. Memory management is one of the major challenges when binding C libraries. In this case, it looks like xmp_get_format_list() returns a pointer to an internal part of memory, which we are not supposed to free().

By default, Vala treats return values as owned, which means the client code claims ownership of the value and is thus also responsible for releasing the memory after usage. To change this, we can use the unowned qualifier:

```
1   [CCode (array_null_terminated = true)]
2   public unowned string[] get_format_list();
```

Compiling and running xmptest again makes the error vanish.

Step 3

In this step, we want to bind xmp_test_module(), a function to check whether libxmp recognizes the format of a given file. The relevant part of xmp.h is

```
1   EXPORT int xmp_test_module(char *, struct xmp_test_info *);
```

This function takes two parameters: a **char*** pointing to the file name and a struct xmp_test_info * pointing to a structure containing module test information. It returns an **int**eger value. From the documentation, we learn, that the second parameter is only written to; hence we should bind this as an out parameter. Let's take a look at how this structure is defined in xmp.h:

```
1   struct xmp_test_info {
2       char name[XMP_NAME_SIZE];      /* Module title */
3       char type[XMP_NAME_SIZE];      /* Module format */
4   };
```

Earlier in that file, you can also find

```
1   #define XMP_NAME_SIZE  64  /* Size of module name and type */
```

This means that the structure contains two fixed-length character buffers, which we could similarly declare in our VAPI. Since both the module title and the module format are zero-terminated strings though, it might make more sense to map them directly to strings. Thus, we add the following lines to libxmp.vapi:

```
1   [CCode (cname = "struct xmp_test_info", cheader_filename =
    "xmp.h", destroy_function = "", has_type_id = false)]
2   public struct TestInfo
3   {
4       public string name;
5       public string type;
6   }
```

The structure gets bound as a Vala struct. Note the two new CCode code attributes destroy_function and has_type_id:

1. Some C structures come with a dedicated function to free the resources taken up by the structure. If you have such a structure, you can specify its destroy_ function here.

2. has_type_id applies to classes, structures, and enumerations, and decides whether to register a corresponding GType with the glib type system.

We can now specify TestInfo as an out parameter for test_module():

```
1   public static int test_module( string path, out TestInfo
    info );
```

Using this from xmptest.vala can look as follows:

```
1   int main( string[] args )
2   {
3       if ( args.length < 2 )
```

```
4       {
5               print( "Usage: %s <module>\n", args[0] );
6               return -1;
7       }
8
9       Xmp.TestInfo info;
10      var valid = Xmp.test_module( args[1], out info );
11
12      if ( valid == 0 )
13      {
14          print( "Valid '%s' module: '%s'\n", info.type,
            info.name );
15      }
16      else
17      {
18          print( "Can't recognize module %s\n", args[1] );
19      }
20
21      return 0;
22  }
```

First, we check whether we received two arguments. If not, we print out a usage string and return -1. Otherwise, we create an Xmp.TestInfo variable to hold the return parameter and then call test_module() with the given path to a module. Based on its return value, we either show the recognized type and name for the module or fail with an appropriate message.

To run this on your machine, you need to have a valid module file. Grab one from the great *AMIGA Music Preservation* site or from the web site *Vanille.de: My AMIGA History*, which is offering many modules composed ages ago by yours truly.

To test our bindings, let's feed xmptest with a valid module:

```
1   $ ./xmptest ~/privates/abgeschlossen/modules/themeofm.mod
2   Valid 'Amiga Protracker/Compatible' module: 'theme-of-magic'
```

And now with an invalid file:

```
1   $ ./xmptest /tmp/foo
2   Can't recognize module '/tmp/foo'
```

Step 4

Let us attempt to load the module now. For this, libxmp offers three
functions in xmp.h:

```
1   EXPORT int xmp_load_module(xmp_context, char *);
2   EXPORT int xmp_load_module_from_memory(xmp_context, void *,
    long);
3   EXPORT int xmp_load_module_from_file(xmp_context, FILE *,
    long);
```

All of them take an xmp_context as first parameter and support loading
from a file path (**char***), a buffer (**void***) in memory, or a POSIX FILE*.

If you take a moment to glimpse over the rest of the functions defined
in xmp.h, you will notice a common API pattern that applies not only to
libxmp: Many C functions operate on a data structure which they take as
the first parameter. While we could map these functions as stand-alone
functions (taking a corresponding Vala struct parameter), this would
not feel very object-oriented. It makes much more sense to bundle the
functions and the data, hence to declare a class.

The xmp_context is the central data structure representing a module
Player. It is created with the function xmp_create_context() and released
with xmp_free_context(xmp_context c). In the header file xmp.h,
xmp_context is being referenced with a **char***—as opposed to a structure
with individual fields—thus being private.

We create a `Player` class as follows:

```
1   [Compact]
2   [CCode (cname = "char", cheader_filename = "xmp.h",
    free_function = " xmp_free_context")]
3   public class Player
4   {
```

We don't use any `GObject` features; hence we can make this a `[Compact]` class. The `CCode` attribute `free_function` applies to classes and allows us to specify a function that gets called when the "destructor" of a class gets called:

```
1       [CCode (cname = "xmp_create_context")]
2       public Player();
3   }
```

We get a class "constructor" by mapping the function `xmp_create_context`. In any VAPI, by default, the "instance" parameter is transferred as the first parameter; hence we do not need to explicitly mention it:

```
1       [CCode (cname = "xmp_load_module")]
2       public int load_module( string path );
3       [CCode (cname = "xmp_load_module_from_memory")]
4       public int load_module_from_memory( uint8[] buffer );
5       [CCode (cname = "xmp_load_module_from_file")]
6       public int load_module_from_file( Posix.FILE file, long
        size );
7   }
```

The three methods to load a module differ only by their parameter lists. Note that we do not need to specify the `xmp_context` parameter, since this is implicitly inserted into the parameter list by Vala, as mentioned earlier.

For the third function, we refer to Posix.FILE. This is a data structure mapping a Posix.FileStream as found in posix.vapi. We are now using an entity defined in another VAPI, so that we have to create a VAPI dependency file called libxmp.deps. This contains one line for every dependency:

```
1    posix
```

To use this class from xmptest, we write the following main():

```
1    int main( string[] args )
2    {
3        if ( args.length < 2 )
4        {
5            print( "Usage: %s <module>\n", args[0] );
6            return -1;
7        }
8
9        var player = new Xmp.Player();
10       var valid = player.load_module( args[1] );
11       if ( valid < 0 )
12       {
13           print( "Can't recognize module '%s'\n", args[1] );
14           return -1;
15       }
16
17       print( "Module %s successfully loaded\n", args[1] );
18
19       return 0;
20   }
```

We create a Player object and call load_module(). If we get a positive return value, it means the Player has successfully loaded our module:

```
1   $ ./xmptest bo_traps.mod
2   Module bo_traps.mod successfully loaded
```

Step 5

As mentioned before, libxmp is the workhorse behind the module player xmp. While it can parse and interpret the module data, it does only render its output to data buffers, that is, there are no audio drivers included.

To have our libxmp binding do something really useful, we need to add three more functions, namely, xmp_start_player(), xml_play_frame(), and xml_get_frame_info():

```
1   EXPORT int  xmp_start_player  (xmp_context, int, int);
2   EXPORT int  xmp_play_frame    (xmp_context);
3   EXPORT void xmp_get_frame_info (xmp_context, struct
    xmp_frame_info *);
```

For xmp_start_player(), there are two **int** parameters: The first denotes the desired sample rate (read: quality) and the second represents a set of format flags. In xmp.h, these format flags are defined as follows:

```
1   #define XMP_FORMAT_8BIT      (1 << 0)
2   #define XMP_FORMAT_UNSIGNED  (1 << 1)
3   #define XMP_FORMAT_MONO      (1 << 2)
```

We could just map them as individual **int** constants; it is slightly more elegant though to map them as an enumeration. We add the following to our VAPI:

```
1   [CCode (cprefix = "XMP_FORMAT_", has_type_id=false)]
2   public enum FormatFlags
```

```
3   {
4       8BIT,
5       UNSIGNED,
6       MONO
7   }
```

With that, we have a proper "type" and can refer to, say, a combination of 8BIT and MONO with Xmp.FormatFlags.8BIT | Xmp.FormatFlags.MONO. The binding for xmp_start_player() then becomes

```
1   [CCode (cname = "xmp_start_player)]
2   public int start( int rate = 44100, FormatFlags format = 0 );
```

Note that we have improved the binding by adding default parameters (which C is lacking).

Binding xmp_play_frame() is straightforward in the VAPI:

```
1   [CCode (cname = "xmp_play_frame")]
2   public int play_frame();
```

No surprises here. Last but not least, we have to bind xmp_get_frame_info(). This function takes a pointer to a struct xmp_frame_info as output parameter, which we have to bind first. It is a structure with 18 fields, of which we only need a few. We add the following declaration to the VAPI:

```
1   [CCode (cname = "struct xmp_frame_info", cheader_filename =
    "xmp.h", destroy_function = "", has_type_id = false)]
2   public struct FrameInfo
3   {
4       [CCode (array_length = false)]
5       uint8[] buffer;
6       int buffer_size;
7       int loop_count;
8   }
```

After xmp_play_frame() has rendered an audio frame, xmp_get_ frame_info() allocates an internal memory block holding this structure with the uint8 audio data in buffer and the number of bytes in buffer_ size. To prevent Vala from expecting an additional parameter for the number of elements contained in the array, we set the array_length code attribute to **false** here. xmp_get_frame_info() is then declared as follows:

```
1  [CCode (cname = "xmp_get_frame_info")]
2  public int get_frame_info( out FrameInfo info );
```

Now we have everything in place to write a program that "plays" the whole module and writes the resulting audio data to stdout. We start with the program from step 4 and add the following code:

```
1  var ok = player.start();
2  if ( ok < 0 )
3  {
4      print( "Can't start playing\n" );
5      return -1;
6  }
```

player_start() might return a negative value. In that case, we exit the main() function by returning -1, indicating an error:

```
1  while ( player.play_frame() == 0 )
2  {
3      Xmp.FrameInfo info;
4      player.get_frame_info( out info );
5      if ( info.loop_count > 0 )
6      {
7          break;
8      }
9      Posix.write( stdout.fileno(), info.buffer, info.
           buffer_size );
10  }
```

In the **while** loop, we call play_frame(), get the frame info with get_frame_info(), and check whether loop_count has become greater than 0. If so, we have reached the end of the module, and the player is about to restart the song. Otherwise, we write the resulting audio data to stdout. Note that stdout is a FileStream and Posix.write needs a file descriptor though.

After compiling this step of xmptest, we can run it:

```
1   $ ./xmpptest ~/privates/abgeschlossen/modules/bo_traps.mod
    >/tmp/mod.raw
2   $ ls -l /tmp/mod.raw
3   -rw-r--r-- 1 mickey  wheel  29804629  1 Feb 16:21
    /tmp/mod.raw
```

The resulting raw file can then be played by any supported command-line audio player, for example, play from the sox package:

```
1   $ play --endian big -e signed-integer -c 2 -b 16 -r 44100 /
    tmp/mod.raw
```

Note that raw files do not contain metadata describing the stream format; hence we need to specify the format (2 channels, 16 bit per sample, sample rate 44100Hz) when calling play.

Example: Binding a GObject-Based Library

As we have seen in the previous chapter, binding a C library can be quite complex. Even for small libraries, there are a lot of ways to introduce compile-time and/or run-time bugs.

Binding libraries based on GObject is much simpler, since these have a unified type system and introspection capabilities: During the build process, the C library can be *scanned* and a metadata file can be generated. Some (scripting) languages read these metadata files at run-time and create bindings on the fly.

While this seamless integration is not possible with Vala, we can still benefit from GObject introspection, thanks to a largely automated binding-creation process. Three steps are necessary:

1. Obtain a *gobject introspection file (GIR)*. This is an XML-derived markup specification that contains descriptions for all entities exposed by the library, such as constants, enumerations, and types.

2. Generate the VAPI with the tool vapigen.

3. Customize the generated bindings by identifying out/ref parameters, adding code attributes, and/or adding custom code.

As an example, we will now bind libgusb, which is a GObject-based wrapper for libusb —a cross-platform library providing simple access to USB devices.

Obtaining the GIR File

Since GIR files are usually created from the source code, you will need to download the source distribution of the desired library. The tool g-ir-scanner reads source files and creates the resulting .gir file.

In the case of libgusb, once the build process has successfully completed, you will find GUsb-1.0. gir in your build directory.

Generating the VAPI

Given a GIR file, the tool vapigen comes into play. As it is part of the Vala distribution, it should already be installed on your machine:

```
1   $ vapigen --pkg=gio-2.0 --library gusb ./GUsb-1.0.gir
```

You should now find the file gusb.vapi in the same directory. Take a moment to glance through this file (if only to value the huge amount of lines we were spared from writing).

Customizing the VAPI

GObject introspection is not perfect: On top of the inevitable amount of small bugs, it does not support all of Vala's language features. Furthermore, for some constructs, there is not enough semantics in the source files. This can lead to missing or wrong

- Nullability specifications

- Parameter directions (i.e., out and ref)

- Ownership qualifiers

- And so on

It also sometimes might not necessarily lead to a very object-oriented API. This is why there is also an opportunity to customize vapigen-created VAPIs.

Note that the first line of a generated VAPI looks similar to this:

```
1   /* gusb.vapi generated by vapigen, do not modify. */
```

For customizing generated VAPIs, vapigen allows weaving your customizations directly into the output. You need to formulate them in a dedicated metadata format. A detailed description of that would unfortunately go beyond the scope of this book.

Please refer to the Vala wiki for details.

Example: Using libgusb

Since we have a binding for libgusb now, let's present an example using it.

The most basic use of libgusb is to retrieve a list of USB devices connected to your machine:

```
1    int main()
2    {
3        var context = new GUsb.Context();
```

We create a new instance of a context, with which we can access all the functionality provided by libgusb:

```
1    var devices = context.get_devices();
```

The method get_devices() returns an array of Device objects. Since this is a GLib.GenericArray, we can't iterate with a standard foreach/in loop:

```
1    devices.foreach( ( device ) => {
```

Instead, we must use the method foreach taking a delegate (or lambda), which is then called for every element in the array:

```
1    var str = "%02x:%02x [%04x:%04x] ".printf(
2        device.get_bus(),
3        device.get_address(),
4        device.get_vid(),
5        device.get_pid()
6        );
```

We construct a string denoting the USB bus number, address, vendor id, and product id:

```
1    device.open();
2    var vendor = device.get_string_descriptor( device.get_
     manufacturer_index() );
```

```
3    var product = device.get_string_descriptor( device.get_
     product_index() );
```

After opening the device, we query the device's manufacturer name and product name:

```
1        str += "%s - %s\n".printf( vendor, product );
2        print( str );
3    } );
4
5    return 0;
6    }
```

We append these names to str before printing it. When compiling this program, remember to tell valac that we are using the package gusb and where to find its .vapi file:

```
1    $ valac --vapidir=. --pkg=gio-2.0 --pkg=gusb ./gusbScan.vala
```

Note that we also have to specify --pkg=gio-2.0, since gusb refers to entities defined in gio but vapigen does not create the corresponding .deps file.

Running gusbScan leads to the following output on my machine (Apple MacBook Pro without any external USB devices attached):

```
1    $ ./gusbScan
2    14:06 [05ac:8289] Apple Inc. - Bluetooth USB Host Controller
3    14:04 [0a5c:4500] Apple Inc. - BRCM20702 Hub
4    14:02 [05ac:025a] Apple Inc. - Apple Internal Keyboard /
     Trackpad
```

Summary

Vala has been designed from the very start to allow for a simple access of external libraries that expose a C API. To use the functionality of such a library, you need to have a Vala API description (VAPI). For libraries based on GObject, such a VAPI can be generated automatically. For all other libraries, they have to be written manually. We have shown how to do both and wrapped up the chapter with an example using libgusb.

Afterword

So Long, and Thanks for All the Fish!

—Douglas Adams, The Hitchhiker's Guide to the Galaxy

Congratulations

Congratulations for making it this far! You have learned how to boost your productivity using Vala in various situations. While the current state of the language itself is pretty stable, the reference implementation for the compiler still has a way to go. You can easily force the compiler to choke on some code pieces—in particular when combining generics, arrays, and delegates.

On the road to version 1.0, this will all hopefully be fixed in the future.

Contribute

If you want to speed up this process and are interested in contributing to an open source programming language project, here are several ways how you can join the Vala community:

- Visit the Vala Wiki, which is a community-hosted documentation.

- Hop over to the IRC channel #vala on irc.freenode. net. IRC clients are available for all kinds of operating systems and platforms. Note that IRC is real-time chat and there might not be someone available right at the very moment you have posted.

© Michael Lauer 2019
M. Lauer, *Introducing Vala Programming*, https://doi.org/10.1007/978-1-4842-5380-9

- Subscribe to the Vala mailing list and post your questions or answers.

- Download the Vala source code and learn how the compiler works.

- Look through the Vala issue tracker and comment on bugs, create new issues, or try to come up with a patch fixing an issue.

While no longer a newborn, Vala is still in an early phase of its life, which means all of us can shape it in the way we want the language to work. Join us!

Closing

I hope you enjoyed reading this introduction into Vala programming. If you have any feedback, suggestions for a follow-up edition, or ideas for a possible sequel about advanced Vala programming, please contact me via e-mail: `michael.lauer@vanille.de`. Take care!

Index

Printed in the United States
by Bookmasters

Printed in the United States
By Bookmasters